TWAYNE'S WORLD AUTHORS SERIES
A Survey of the World's Literature

FRANCE

Maxwell A. Smith, Guerry Professor of French, Emeritus
The University of Chattanooga
Former Visiting Professor in Modern Languages
The Florida State University
EDITOR

Antonin Artaud

TWAS 492

Antonin Artaud

ANTONIN ARTAUD

By JULIA F. COSTICH

University of Kentucky

CARNE...
LIVINGSTON...
SALISBURY, N. C. 28144

CARNEGIE LIBRARY
LIVINGSTONE COLLEGE
SALISBURY, N. C. 28144

TWAYNE PUBLISHERS
A DIVISION OF G. K. HALL & CO., BOSTON

Copyright © 1978 by G. K. Hall & Co.

Published in 1978 by Twayne Publishers,
A Division of G. K. Hall & Co.
All Rights Reserved

Printed on permanent/durable acid-free paper and bound
in the United States of America

First Printing

Library of Congress Cataloging in Publication Data

Costich, Julia F.
Antonin Artaud.

(Twayne's world author series ; TWAS 492 :
France)
Bibliography: p. 129-30
Includes index.
1. Artaud, Antonin, 1896-1948—Criticism and
interpretation. I. Title.
PO2601.R677Z632   1978   842'.9'12   78-4641
ISBN 0-8057-6333-3

842.912
ar 785

Contents

107198

About the Author

Julia Field Costich received her B.A. from Duke University and her M.A. and Ph.D. from the University of Kentucky. She has published articles on French literature in *Dada/Surrealism*, *French Review* and *Romance Notes*, and she is the author of a study of the Surrealist poet Benjamin Péret which will be published by the University of North Carolina Press. Dr. Costich has taught at the University of Kentucky; she is Editorial Assistant for French Forum Publications.

Preface

The writing of Antonin Artaud is inseparable from his physical existence in the world. While his earliest poetry resembles the efforts of his contemporaries, the fact that it is typical of its time makes this production aberrant in the context of Artaud's literary creation. After 1924, Artaud's poetry, prose, theater and letters reflect a conscious decision to express the fragmented, painful nature of his thought process. The historical and literary figures who appear in Artaud's texts, as well as his fictional creations, are avatars of his own tormented being.

In the worlds of literature and the performing arts, "Artaud" has become a code word for an ill-defined, rather free-form amalgam of violence, obscenity, and revolt. His theater has become a matter of fashion with general associations with the *gauchisme* and student movements of the 1960s and, more recently, with the *Tel Quel* group. Artaud is alluded to far more frequently than he is read, and his work has been reduced to a pair of terms: "cruelty" and "double." In the late 1970s, his texts run the risk of being discarded when literary fashion moves on to a new hero.

The purpose of this volume, then, is to describe and discuss what is actually there: Artaud's writings as they appear in the first fourteen volumes of his complete works, which have been published by Gallimard in an authoritative edition by his appointed editor, Mme. Paule Thévenin. Artaud's poetry, prose, theater and letters will be treated in roughly chronological order, with major emphasis on his two theaters (the Alfred Jarry Theater and the Theater of Cruelty), his quest for a culture, and the unique texts produced after his release from mental institutions.

It is hoped that the interested reader will be inspired to approach some of Artaud's texts on his own, either in the original French or in the excellent translation by Helen Weaver. These writings are not to be read casually as a new venture in sensationalism; they are often difficult, occasionally outrageous, violent, or even humorous, but their intent is always serious.

In view of the diversity of the public which this volume hopes to reach, little attempt has been made to place Artaud in literary, theatrical, or philosophical contexts. It is up to the authentically interested reader to find Artaud's place in his or her studies.

I wish to thank *Dada/Surrealism* for permission to repeat here some of the contents of my article on *Héliogabale*. Further thanks are due Professor Virginia A. La Charité, whose assistance and suggestions have been invaluable in the preparation of this manuscript.

JULIA F. COSTICH

Lexington, Kentucky

Chronology

1896	Born in Marseilles (September 4).
1901	Nearly dies of meningitis. Several childhood vacations in Smyrna, Greece, with grandmother.
1910	Founds a schoolboy poetry review while attending the Marist College in Marseilles. Publishes texts under the pseudonym Louis des Attides.
1915	Parents send him to a sanitarium at La Rouguière, near Marseilles. Suffers from headaches, physical depression, and stuttering.
1916	Is drafted into the Third Infantry Regiment; discharged after nine months for ill health.
1918– 1920	Two years at Chanet clinic near Neuchâtel, Switzerland. Continues to write and paint.
1920	Moves to Paris. Lives with Dr. Edouard Toulouse at his Villejuif clinic.
1921	First theatrical role in Lugné-Poe's company. Later joins Charles Dullin's theatrical group, L'Atelier. Meets Génica Athanasiou.
1922	Many theatrical roles. Attempt at detoxification from opium addiction.
1923	Founds the personal review *Bilboquet; Tric-trac du ciel* published. Begins correspondence with Jacques Rivière. Frequents the Rue Blomet group.
1924	Film roles (through 1934). Joins Surrealist group. Publication of *Correspondance avec Jacques Rivière*. Father dies; mother moves to Paris.
1925	Director of Centrale Surréaliste; edits a number of *La Révolution Surréaliste*. Publication of *L'Ombilic des limbes* and *Le Pése-nerfs*.
1926	Leaves Surrealist group. Founds Théâtre Alfred Jarry with Roger Vitrac and Robert Aron.
1927– 1929	Performances of Théâtre Alfred Jarry.

1927	Publication of *La Coquille et le clergyman* (scenario) and *L'Art et la mort*. Breaks with Génica Athanasiou. *A la grande nuit ou le Bluff surr*éaliste.
1928	Repudiates film of *La Coquille et le clergyman*.
1931	*Le Moine* (translation). Preparations for Theater of Cruelty. "Manifeste du Théâtre de la cruauté." Contact with German filmmakers (early thirties).
1933	"Le Théâtre et la peste." Association with Anaïs Nin.
1934	*Héliogabale, ou l'Anarchiste couronné.*
1935	Seventeen performances of *Les Cenci* (May). Failure of Theater of Cruelty.
1936	January-November in Mexico. Lectures and newspaper articles. "D'un voyage au pays des Tarahumaras." Brief engagement to Cécile Schramme.
1937	*Les Nouvelles Révélations de l'Etre.* Travel to Ireland; on return, is arrested and sent to the asylum at Quatre-Mares (Rouen).
1938	*Le Théâtre et son double.* Transferred to Sotteville-lès-Rouen, then to Sainte-Anne asylum (Paris).
1939	Transferred to Ville-Evrard asylum; diagnosed as incurable schizophrenic.
1943	Moved to Rodez (Aveyron) in the care of Dr. Gaston Ferdière. Period of religious fervor. Begins writing many letters and texts.
1946	*Lettres de Rodez.* Released from Rodez into the care of Dr. Achille Delmas at Ivry, near Paris. Benefit exhibition and reading at Sarah Bernhardt Theater.
1947	*Van Gogh, le suicidé de la société; Artaud le Mômo; Ci-gît, suivi de la Culture indienne; Pour en finir avec le jugement de dieu.* Exhibit of Artaud's portraits and drawings in Paris.
1948	"Tête-à-tête" performance at Vieux Colombier Theater. Dies at Ivry, March 4.
1952	*Vie et mort de Satan le Feu.*
1956	Gallimard publishes Volume I of Artaud's *Oeuvres complètes*. Thirteen other volumes are projected.
1973	Cérisy Colloquium on Artaud.

CHAPTER 1

A Life of Crisis

I *Childhood and Adolescence*

BETWEEN his birth on September 4, 1896, and his arrival in Paris
in 1920, Artaud's life was marked by a series of crises which were
to set a pattern for his existence. From the period of the Theater of
Cruelty (1931–35) onward, his life was a single sustained crisis, a state
of physical and mental emergency which profoundly conditioned his
written work. His childhood experience includes a serious case of
meningitis at the age of five, a near-drowning at ten, and the death of
several siblings, most notably an infant sister, Germaine, whose
death haunts him in later years.

Artaud's grandmothers were sisters named Chili (variously spelled
Schilley or Chilé) who lived in Smyrna, Greece; as a child, Artaud
vacationed with them and learned some Greek. His father, who bore
the forbidding name Antoine-Roi, was a shipmerchant; he appears to
have had little influence on the young Antonin. On the other hand,
he was very close to his mother, *née* Euphrasie Nalpas, and continued to live with her as a young man after his father's death in 1924.

As an adult, Artaud remembered childhood with bitterness:

Je me demandais pourquoi j'étais là et ce que c'était que d'être là. . . . Les
coups, les calottes, les réprimandes, les semonces sempiternelles à propos de
rien et de tout. . . . C'est ainsi que je fus enfant dans le scandale de mon
moi.[1]

While he was a student at the Marist College in Marseilles, Artaud
began a poetry review with friends and wrote verse under the
pseudonym "Louis des Attides." He painted, drew, and read widely,
especially the works of Baudelaire and Edgar Allen Poe.[2] At the age of
nineteen, Artaud fell into a deep depression during which he de-

stroyed his early writings, liquidated his library, and severed contacts
with his friends. His alarmed parents sent him to a nearby sanitarium,
La Rouguière, for a few months—the first of a long chain of institutional experiences which marks his life. Upon his return to Marseilles, Artaud was drafted into the army, but after nine months' service
he was discharged for reasons of health (according to Artaud, for
sleepwalking). The next two years found him intermittently in three
other sanitoria, but he still suffered from intense headaches, depression, and other psychosomatic disorders. His parents thought that
the Chanet clinic of Dr. Dardel, near Neuchâtel, Switzerland, would
effect a definitive cure, and during the two years he spent there, he
continued to read and draw. A brief return to Marseilles in 1919
found Artaud full of plans for his first serious theatrical project: he
hoped to set up a theater in a factory. While this plan never came to
fruition, it was apparent that he would never enter the family
shipchandlers' business, so his parents sent him to Paris, where he
might begin his chosen career in the arts.

II *Early Paris Years*

Artaud began his Parisian life in March 1920, when he arrived at
the home of Dr. Edouard Toulouse, the director of an asylum at
Villejuif. According to Mme Toulouse's account, her husband immediately recognized in their new boarder "un être tout à fait
exceptionnel, de cette race qui donne des Baudelaire, des Nerval et
des Nietzsche."[3] Artaud found in Dr. Toulouse not only a sympathetic medical counselor but also an intermittent employer. As the
editorial secretary for Toulouse's review *Demain*, Artaud had a
ready-made publishing outlet for poetry, essays, and reviews of
literature, art, and theater;[4] he also edited and prefaced a collection
of the doctor's texts. Artaud remained in Toulouse's care after he left
Villejuif for Passy; it was not until around 1930 that he transferred his
medical loyalties to Dr. René Allendy.

Meanwhile, Artaud's associations with the world of the arts in Paris
grew more numerous and varied. He met Max Jacob, who was a great
facilitator for aspiring writers in the 1920s and introduced Artaud to
potential colleagues and publishers. Among the diverse reviews in
which Artaud's poetry and essays appeared, aside from *La Criée* in
Marseilles, are *Action, Le Mercure de France, Les Cahiers du Sud,
Images de Paris*, and *L'Ere nouvelle*. His first collection of poetry, *Le
Tric-trac du ciel (Heavenly Backgammon)*, which he later re-

pudiated, was published in 1923; small in every respect, it consisted of only eight poems and appeared in a limited edition of one hundred copies.

More important at this time is Artaud's work in the theater. Through the director Firmin Gémier, he met Charles Dullin, one of the most innovative men of the theater of his time; Artaud was active in Dullin's Théâtre de l'Atelier until 1924. Admiring Dullin's moral qualities as well as his artistic principles, Artaud collaborated in set decoration and costume design and acted in many of the Atelier's productions. The only full-fledged love affair of Artaud's life dates from this period: Génica Athanasiou was a comrade in the Atelier and the object of a remarkable correspondence from Artaud which charts the course of their relationship until their final break in 1927.[5]

Because experimental theater does not pay a living wage, Artaud turned to film in order to become self-supporting. His uncle, Louis Nalpas, was influential in the French film industry and seems to have helped him begin this career. Even so, he was very poor, and anecdotes tell of his sleeping in the theater itself when the rent of a hotel room was beyond his resources. After his father's death in 1924, he lived with his mother in the suburb of Passy.

Artaud was still in the precarious physical and mental state which marks his adolescence, and since 1919 he had been taking both laudanum and opium to alleviate mental anguish and physical pain. The crisis in his working relationships with Dullin and others, as well as his troubled affair with Génica Athanasiou, are all closely tied to his intermittent painful attacks although no clear-cut causal relationship can be detected.

Correspondance avec Jacques Rivière, the first text by Artaud to attract wide attention, derives from this experience of pain. His correspondence with Rivière, the editor of the prestigious *Nouvelle Revue Française*, is a paradox, for it is the successful account of a literary failure. Artaud submitted poetry which Rivière, as editor, rejected, but they continued to correspond on the subjects of poetry and Artaud's special relationship to writing. Rivière and Artaud met several times, and the *Nouvelle Revue Française* published their correspondence later in 1924.

The year 1924 marks another important beginning for Artaud: his association with the newly formed Surrealist group, led by André Breton. Artaud already knew the artists of the Rue Blomet group, particularly Michel Leiris, Elie Lascaux, and Joan Miró, and he formed a lasting friendship with André Masson. Like Artaud, these artists were to become "official" Surrealists for a time, but would eventually leave the movement. Thinking the Surrealists were as possessed as he by the spirit of revolt, Artaud gave all his energies to the movement in early 1925. Not only was he the first director of the "Surrealist Central Bureau" at 15, rue de Grenelle, but he edited the third number of the official Surrealist organ, *La Révolution Surréaliste*. Most of the series of "open letters" in this number are written by Artaud, and the collective title, "1925: Fin de l'ère chrétien" ("1925: End of the Christian Era"), reflects his confident enthusiasm.

Artaud's first two important collections, *L'Ombilic des limbes (The Navel of Limbo*, 1925) and *Le Pèse-Nerfs (The Nerve Scale*, 1925), date from this period; *L'Art et la mort (Art and Death*, 1927) also includes texts written while Artaud was part of the Surrealist group. His association with the Surrealists continued until November 1926, with more tenuous contact until 1928. Among the reasons for Artaud's break with Surrealism—Breton's antipathy toward theater and Artaud's inability to work with a group are obvious contributing factors—the most significant is a profound difference in attitude toward life itself. The Surrealists generally enjoyed excellent health; they loved life and wanted to change political, poetic, and social structures, while Artaud sought a total metaphysical transformation of the conditions of human existence. Artaud's first priority throughout his life is a radical reading of Rimbaud's famous dictum, "changer la vie" ("to change life"), for his own physical existence was unbearable. While Surrealist writing is full of corporeal change, this motif appears in a playful tone, while for Artaud, the physical rearrangement of the body was a necessary precondition for any meaningful amelioration of the human condition.

It is not surprising that the Surrealists' adherence to the Communist party (which was only temporary, as it turned out) and their lasting insistence on political revolution alienated Artaud. His public exclusion, announced by the brochure *Au grand jour* (1927), was answered by his own publication of *A la grande nuit ou le Bluff surréaliste (In Broad Night or The Surrealist Bluff)* in June of the same year. Artaud had other projects well under way by this time and was making a name for himself apart from any political or artistic movement.

III   *Two Theaters*

Artaud's first attempt to form an independent theater grew out of his frustration with the theater of the 1920s. With the playwrights Roger Vitrac, who had also been associated with Surrealism, and Robert Aron, and with the financial support of Mme Allendy, Artaud announced the founding of the Alfred Jarry Theater in a manifesto published in the *Nouvelle Revue Française* of November 1926. After a number of setbacks, the first performance took place on June 1 and 2, 1927, with plays by all three collaborators, including Artaud's *Ventre brûlé ou La Mère folle (Burned Belly or The Mad Mother)*, which has unfortunately been lost. The second performance, on January 14, 1928, was deliberately provocative: along with a showing of Pudovkin's forbidden film of Gorki's *The Mother*, the company performed an unauthorized version of Act III of Claudel's *Partage de midi (Noontime Division)*, accompanied by a negative comment on the author by Artaud. On June 2, 1928, the staging of Strindberg's *Dream Play* with the support of the Swedish Embassy aroused the violent opposition of the Surrealists, who felt that Artaud was in collusion with a venal Establishment; the "Dream Play Affair" marks Artaud's final break with the movement. Before the Alfred Jarry Theater closed for lack of funds, it gave three performances of Vitrac's *Victor, ou Les Enfants au pouvoir (Victor, or Power to the Children)* on December 24 and 28 and January 5, 1929.

Artaud's activity in the cinema continued on two fronts during this period. His roles in productions of widely varying quality were virtually his only source of income; the best-known is that of Brother Matthieu Krassien in Dreyer's *The Passion of Joan of Arc*. Artaud's scripts went unproduced with the exception of *La Coquille et le clergyman (The Seashell and the Clergyman*, 1927), and this single success proved a personal failure. The direction of Artaud's scenario by Germaine Dulac was, he felt, a terrible distortion of his intentions. At the February 18 premiere, he and Robert Desnos broke the silence of the screening with a loud "conversation" in which he called Mme Dulac a cow. In film, as in the theater, independent production seemed the only solution. In 1929, Artaud hoped to found a new cinematic company, again with the financial support of Mme Allendy; although this plan was never executed, it does indicate Artaud's continuing need for a creative forum of his own.[6]

Artaud's energies returned to the theater in 1931. The appearance that summer of a Balinese theatrical troupe at the Colonial Exposition confirmed his growing belief in the primary importance of physical gesture in the creation of a truly metaphysical theater. From April 1931 to the spring of 1932, Artaud worked closely with the theatrical company of the well-known director Louis Jouvet and expressed a strong desire to be given a position which would free him from financial dependence on film roles. The answer lay in the founding of a new, radically different theater based on highly innovative, publicly announced dramatic principles which would attract the public's interest and the financial support essential to such an elaborate venture. Several of the articles and lectures which were to be included in *Le Théâtre et son double* (*Theater and Its Double*, 1938)—"Sur le théâtre balinais" ("On Balinese Theater," 1931), "La Mise-en-scène et la métaphysique" ("Staging and Metaphysics," 1931), "Le Théâtre alchimique" ("Alchemical Theater," 1932), "Premier Manifeste du Théâtre de la Cruauté," ("First Manifesto of the Theater of Cruelty," 1932), "Le Théâtre de la cruauté" ("The Theater of Cruelty," 1933), and "Le Théâtre et la peste" ("Theater and the Plague," 1933)—date from this period.

Artaud hoped to have the patronage of the *Nouvelle Revue Française*, but untimely publicity of this project led to its failure and, for a time, to a breach between Artaud and the staff of the journal. In those years of financial crisis, money failed to appear in any quantity, forcing Artaud to postpone the realization of his scheme from season to season. His disappointment turned to bitterness when he saw established directors successfully incorporating what he insisted were his own ideas into their productions. He lived on the meager revenues of two books: a French translation and adaptation of Matthew Lewis's *The Monk* (*Le Moine*, 1931) and *Héliogabale, ou l'Anarchiste couronné* (*Heliogabalus, or The Crowned Anarchist*, 1934), a historically based text which incorporates aspects of the theory of cruelty. The failure of two attempts at detoxification (1932 and 1935) and continuing poverty brought Artaud to despair of his future before the first performance of the Theater of Cruelty took place in May 1935.

In *Les Cenci* (*The Cenci*), the only play produced by the Theater of Cruelty, Artaud had found an unusual vehicle for his theatrical innovations. Adapting texts by Shelley and Stendhal, designing the complex staging of the play, directing, and playing the male lead, Artaud had his wish for independence—but under such exiguous conditions that rehearsal time was virtually nonexistent and the theater itself utterly inappropriate. Artaud suffered from the generally negative critical reception given the play, both personally and financially, for the lukewarm public response placed the future of his cherished project in serious jeopardy. He began his defense of the Theater of Cruelty by regretting the constraints placed on his conceptions of the production, especially those imposed by Iya Abdy, who, as co-financier and female lead, succeeded in dictating the conditions of her performance. Then he turned to the attack: he wrote to Louis Jouvet that the fault was not in his ideas, but in the society which stifled them. Bourgeois capitalism must give way: "1° parce qu'il n'a plus en lui de quoi faire face aux nécessités catastrophiques de l'heure; 2° parce qu'il est *immoral* étant bâti exclusivement sur le gain et sur l'argent" (III, 256).[7] For Artaud, *Les Cenci* and the profound metaphysical significance of the Theater of Cruelty had been totally misinterpreted by the French public because they lacked a true culture.

IV *Search, Research, and Travel*

Rather than continue an effort to convert the French public to such a view of culture, Artaud sought it elsewhere: in Mexico, where the indigenous culture promised an audience capable of understanding the Theater of Cruelty. Before his departure for Mexico, Artaud arranged with Jean Paulhan to have his essays on the theater published and signed a contract to write a work entitled *Satan.* The latter volume was never completed; texts found by Serge Berna and published under the title *Vie et mort de Satan le Feu* (*Life and Death of the Late /Fire Satan*, 1952) appear to relate to this project. Artaud was convinced that Mexico held great promise for him, and he wrote Paulhan: "je sens que quelque chose d'important, peut-être de sensationnel peut sortir de tout cela" (VIII, 337).[8] Natural magic, the solar cult, the visions offered by peyote made him foresee an experience of cultural and personal unification.

Penniless as always, Artaud finally obtained an official mission from the French Office of National Education and left from Antwerp on January 10, 1936. At an intermediate stop in Havana, his enthusiasm undiminished, he wrote of "signs," including a small dagger given him by a Cuban "magician," which confirmed his hopes. Once in Mexico City however, his official round of lectures brought him into contact with the reality of contemporary Mexico: a civilization largely modeled on Western Europe, preaching Marxism and scorning indigenous culture. In his lectures at the university, he emphasized the importance of a surrealism separated from Marxism and of the activity of young directors like himself.

In order to experience traditional Mexican culture, Artaud planned an expedition to the land of the Tarahumara Indians, an isolated tribe of the Sierra Madre. His chronic lack of funds posed an obstacle, but a petition by Mexican intellectuals on his behalf finally made the realization of this project possible, and he left for the Sierra Madre at the end of August. Artaud's experiences among the Tarahumaras mark a turning point in his life. His written accounts begin even before his return to Mexico City at the beginning of October, and they span twelve years; the last, *Tutuguri, le soleil noir* (*Tutuguri, the Black Sun*), was written shortly before his death. His interpretation ranges from the fervently positive to the violently negative, but it never loses an apocalyptic note, which indicates the great importance of this experience in his life.

Artaud returned to Paris filled with a messianic conviction that only the metaphysical advent of traditional culture would save European society from destruction, but despite the vehemence of his discourse, he found only an apathetic audience. His reaction was double and apparently paradoxical: while he grew more intensely involved with esotericism, especially numerology, astrology, and the tarot, he also sought the stability of a remarkably bourgeois marriage with a young Belgian woman, Cécile Schramme. The latter effort came to a predictable end when, during a lecture in Brussels, Artaud insulted his audience, thereby convincing his fiancée's father of his unsuitability as a son-in-law.

Artaud acquired a strange knotted cane from the wife of the painter Kristian Tony, and he became convinced that it was the lost "cane of Saint Patrick" which dated from the time of Jesus and had been used to drive the serpents from Ireland. His writings became increasingly apocalyptic: on the one hand, he was certain that great changes had taken place to make him an entirely new person, while on the other hand, he expected the imminent end of the world. "My name must disappear," he said, and he published anonymously *Les Nouvelles Révélations de l'Etre* (*The New Revelations of Being*, 1937) and "D'un voyage au pays des Tarahumaras" ("Of a voyage to the land of the Tarahumaras," 1937). At this time, André Breton, although admittedly skeptical of Artaud's predictions, became his close friend again.

The "cane of Saint Patrick" led Artaud's thoughts toward Ireland; perhaps he would find there the true culture he had sought in

Mexico. His demeanor became prophetic: he spoke as a heroic figure carrying the word of God. The destruction of the world which he predicted would not be total, but rather would devastate the false, the nonessential, and give way to a limitless existence. In Ireland, where he arrived on August 14, 1937, Artaud continued to prophesy in this manner through Cobh, Galway, Kilroman, and Dublin. His behavior finally so disturbed the religious community at the hostel of St. John of God that he was arrested on September 18. His precious cane was confiscated—stolen, he said, by Dublin authorities—and, without resources, he was deported on September 29 aboard the ship *Washington*.

Artaud's legal status was precarious enough at this point, but an episode on board ship determined his terrible fate for the next nine years. According to Artaud, he was standing peacefully looking out a porthole when a steward and a chief mechanic, armed with monkey wrenches, came in brusquely and threatened him (in the *Lettres de Rodez* he qualifies their movements as an assassination attempt). Alone and unsupported, he attempted to defend himself and was placed in a straitjacket by shipboard authorities.

V The Asylum Years

On his arrival at Le Havre (September 30), Artaud was imprisoned, first at the asylum at Quatre-Mares, near Rouen, then, in early 1938, at Sotteville-lès-Rouen. Even his family did not know his whereabouts for many weeks. On April 12, 1938, he was transferred to Sainte-Anne, the famous mental hospital near Paris, where his friends Roger Blin and Robert Desnos found him in a deplorable condition, "speaking like Saint Jerome." He would not have the chance to write at all until his move to another asylum, Ville-Evrard, on February 27, 1939, and it was not until 1943, with his installation at Rodez in "Free France," that his creative work began again.

Ironically, it was in 1938, when he was in the darkest period of his asylum years, that *Le Théâtre et son double*, undoubtedly Artaud's best known work, was published. At Ville-Evrard, he was judged to be an incurable schizophrenic and spent long periods in the "security quarters," in solitary confinement. The horror of Artaud's misery, his unsympathetic treatment and virtual starvation, are vividly described in his later letters.

For thirty years a violent argument has raged between those who find Artaud's incarceration to have been justified—primarily psychiatrists and partisans of his family—and those who revile this action as the vicious and oppressive murder of a brilliant mind. The question is not whether Artaud's mental state matched the diagnosis of psychosis, for unquestionably it did, but whether this diagnosis itself is a valid social instrument or a means to suppress and stigmatize those who threaten the bourgeois social order.

These conflicting points of view focus on Artaud's internment under the care of Dr. Gaston Ferdière at Rodez. Desnos hoped that the new environment would be beneficial to Artaud, since Dr. Ferdière was known for his work with art therapy. Artaud arrived at Rodez in southwest France on February 11, 1943. A positive index of his mental state is found in the number and variety of texts which he began to write in the fall and winter of 1943: "Le Rite du peyotl" ("The Peyote Rite") and other texts concerning his Mexican experience, translations of Lewis Carroll, Robert Southwell, and Edgar Allen Poe, an essay on Ronsard, and the voluminous correspondence later published as *Lettres de Rodez*. Ferdière's use of shock treatments and chemotherapy, which Artaud violently resented, are credited by some for this return to creative activity and condemned by others as gratuitous torture.

Artaud appears to have had periods of deep Christian fervor during his internment; he frequently expresses a close identification with Jesus. For a time, his letters are signed with the childhood nickname "Nanaqui" or with "Antonin Nalpas" (his mother's maiden name), and he declares that Antonin Artaud is dead. By 1945, however, he has rejected Christianity as radically as he embraced it, saying that he always abominated Christ and was "converted" by black magic. His preoccupation with sorcerers and cabalistic plots continued until his death, as did the use of invented language in the form of written and oral incantations.

Artaud's fervent desire to be released from Rodez was supported by the painter Jean Dubuffet and his wife, by Marthe Robert, and by the playwright Arthur Adamov, whose visit to Rodez prompted the initiation of official proceedings. Artaud was given conditional freedom to spend time outside the asylum in a hotel in nearby Espalion, and, after a brief return to Rodez, he moved on May 26 to his final home on the grounds of a rest home at Ivry on the outskirts of Paris.

VI   *The Final Years*

At Ivry, Artaud lived in a cottage which was supposed to have once been the residence of Gérard de Nerval, one of Artaud's favorite poets. Although he was under the general supervision of Dr. Achille

Delmas, he was free to come and go as he pleased. Because his freedom was conditional upon the assurance that he would have some means of support, on June 6, 1946, an auction was held which included paintings and manuscripts by virtually every major French artist of the time, from Picasso to Sartre. It brought revenues of more than a million francs, and a gala benefit at the Sarah Bernhardt Theater on the following evening further augmented the fund.

From the time of his return to Paris until a few days before his death, Artaud's written output was prodigious. He wrote constantly: on buses, in cafés, on the fireplace mantel in his cottage. His return to active life was accompanied by considerable publicity, and, as his name was already well known in literary circles, his activities attracted a great deal of attention, appreciative or bemused. Artaud's January 13, 1947, lecture at the Vieux-Colombier Theater, entitled "Tête-à-tête," was crowded with both friends and curiosity-seekers. After twelve years of silence, Artaud returned to the stage to give his most memorable performance, for what was billed as a lecture rapidly turned into a manifestation of the Theater of Cruelty. Again, however, Artaud's most heartfelt efforts were followed by disappointment, for his readings of some of his most violent poetry came to an abrupt halt, confusing the already startled audience. Finally, André Gide mounted the stage and embraced Artaud, bringing the evening to a nominally satisfactory conclusion. But in the midst of the performance, Artaud had suddenly realized the futility of such an event, and found the French public so corrupt that only military violence could have an effect on its deadened consciousness.[9] From then on, he would become a human theater in himself, aiming a verbal machine gun at the world.

In the same month, Artaud visited an exposition of Van Gogh's paintings at the Orangerie. He found in the painter a mind and a life very like his own, and he was revolted by the various psychiatric evaluations which were discussed in accounts of the exposition. Defending himself as well as Van Gogh with an attack against the society which reduces the genius to suicide, he wrote *Van Gogh, le suicidé de la société* (*Van Gogh, Society's Suicide*, 1947). It is ironic that this violent, lyrical work was awarded the Sainte-Beuve prize for literature, which gave Artaud an unwanted official status.

Other texts from this period of incessant writing are *Artaud le Mômo, Ci-gît suivi de La Culture indienne* (*Here Lies, followed by Indian Culture*), and the largely unpublished texts collectively entitled *Suppôts et Suppliciations* (*Dupes and Tortures*). An exhibit of portraits and drawings by Artaud at the Galerie Pierre (July 4–20, 1947) was accompanied by a reading on July 19. Plans were under way for the publication of Artaud's complete works by Gallimard; he wrote the preamble as early as 1946, and officially confided in Paule Thévenin the responsibility of editing the texts. Her painstaking, loyal work over a period of nearly thirty years has repaid his confidence in her.

Artaud had suffered physically throughout his life, and now violent intestinal pains and hemorrhages curbed his activity. Although his distress was officially attributed to prolonged malnutrition, Paule Thévenin has indicated that he suffered from an inoperable cancer of the rectum, while others insist that his pain was largely psychosomatic and he died of an overdose of chloral hydrate. Strong doses of laudanum, as well as the drug which some say caused his death, were finally augmented with opium when the gravity of his illness was officially recognized. Although Artaud was never told the specific diagnosis, his exacerbated awareness of his body, the product of years of suffering, provided him with insight into the nature of his disease: his last texts are full of references to the afflicted area.[10]

Artaud's final major project, a radio broadcast of *Pour en finir avec le jugement de dieu* (*To End God's Judgment*, 1948), was also the last in a long series of frustrations which scar his life. After painstaking rehearsals with the assistance of Roger Blin, Maria Casarès, and Paule Thévenin, the performance was taped for broadcast on February 2, 1948, but the director of the French radio network, Wladimir Porché, intervened to forbid the broadcast despite violent protests and the resignation of the director of dramatic and literary programming. The ultimate audience was limited to those who attended two private performances on February 5 and 23, 1948. Artaud's disappointment at the fate of *Pour en finir avec le jugement de dieu* was heightened by dissatisfaction with the actual performance:

> Là où est la *machine*
> c'est toujours le gouffre et le néant
> il y a une interposition technique qui déforme et annihile
> ce que l'on fait. (XIII, 146)[11]

In February 1948, after the radio project had failed, Artaud hoped to return to the theater—a poem entitled "Le Théâtre de la cruauté" (1948) comes at the very end of his life. Growing weaker during the month, he announced that he had nothing more to say and would no longer write, although he would continue to draw. While he had frequently proclaimed that he would escape death, that dying was a fraud perpetrated by sinister occult forces or human weaknesses, he seems to have known that his own end was near. On the morning of March 4, 1948, a gardener at Ivry entered Artaud's cottage and found him dead, seated at the foot of his bed, a shoe in his hand.

CHAPTER 2

A Poetry of Fragmentation

A RTAUD'S early writings are the conventional poems and prefaces of an aspirant to fame in the Parisian literary world. *Le Tric-trac du ciel (Heavenly Backgammon,* 1923) is not included as the first group of texts in Volume I of Artaud's complete works; in his 1946 preface, he finds that it "ne me représente en aucune façon" (I, 9).[1] The style he attempts to perfect in his earliest texts is a mixture of Gothic Romanticism, Symbolism, and the influences of Baudelaire and Poe—the style which marked a poem as acceptable for one of the dominant literary reviews of the time. In 1923, a month after his first letter to Jacques Rivière, Artaud renounces the poetry which exists as a function of literary tradition in favor of a poetry of his living being. His letters to Rivière efface the texts which were their original subject, leaving in their wake a new mode of discontinuous and fragmented expression which follows the anguishing experience of one who finds himself incapable of normal intellectual activity.

Rivière turned down Artaud's poetry, but he expressed an interest in meeting the author. As their correspondence continued over a period of more than a year, Rivière proposed the publication of their letters in the *Nouvelle Revue Française*, and they were published in a separate volume by the *NFR* in 1927.

In a letter written at the end of May 1923, after his first meeting with Rivière, Artaud arrives at a formulation which describes his mental state and its relationship to verbal expression:

Je souffre d'une effroyable maladie de l'esprit. Ma pensée m'abandonne à tous les degrés. Depuis le fait simple de la pensée jusqu'au fait extérieur de sa matérialisation dans les mots. Mots, formes de phrases, directions intérieures de la pensée, réactions simples de l'esprit, je suis à la poursuite constante de mon être intellectuel. Lors donc que *je peux saisir une forme,* si imparfaite soit-elle, je la fixe dans la crainte de perdre toute la pensée. Je suis au-dessous de moi-même, je le sais, j'en souffre, mais n'y consens dans la peur de ne pas mourir tout à fait. (I, 30)[2]

Hence, two important discontinuities distinguish Artaud from other writers: an intermittent absence of thought and an inability to express thought verbally. Each poem has the importance of an island in the blank sea of absence. After the futile attempts to fashion recognizable poetry from brief interludes of successful thought, Artaud turns to a style which matches the fissures and fragments of his mental state. Thus, the *Correspondance* is not only the announcement of a turning point in Artaud's verbal expression but it is also an introduction to *L'Ombilic des limbes (The Navel of Limbo)* and *Le Pèse-nerfs (The Nerve Scale)*.

As the correspondence with Rivière continues, Artaud insists with increasing frequency that he is unique among his contemporaries and that his suffering gives his creations a special necessity. He is aware that his contact with Rivière is a privileged public enactment of crisis in which he must defend himself by repulsing false diagnoses and comparisons. When Rivière suggests that he is like Breton, Tzara, or Reverdy, he retorts that "leur âme n'est pas physiologiquement atteinte, elle ne l'est pas substantiellement" (I, 50),[3] as is his own. Rivière finally realizes that while even he suffers from doubt and inadequacy, he is ultimately certain of his own reality as it is manifested in his own powers, but this confidence is denied to Artaud. Artaud's authority has entirely different roots: "Je suis un homme qui a beaucoup souffert de l'esprit, et à ce titre j'ai le *droit* de parler" (I, 38).[4] The painful experience of destroyed thought, as well as physical distress, is not only his justification but his inspiration.

In the *Correspondance* and the three collections of poetry and prose which follow, Artaud reiterates his view of the cosmos and of himself. He perceives an evil force ruling the world, a force of such malevolent grandeur that it surpasses the theologies of existing cults. A universal life force animates the individual, and he feels the impetus of this force within himself. Through his writing, Artaud materializes the power of this dynamism and thereby participates in the universal life; if he is unable to do so, he experiences anguish and paralysis because he feels cut off from all life. His mind is a faulty mechanism (I, 104), his soul, an ill-adjusted clockwork—physical death is less fearful than the intermittent living death of mind and body deprived of communication with themselves and the world.

The metaphysical aspect of Artaud's worldview becomes a more frequent subject in the 1930s and 1940s when the revelation of universal cruelty and malevolent force in the world takes on dramatic and poetic urgency. In all his texts, Artaud's dual preoccupation is with himself and with the cosmic force; historical figures and contemporary friends suffer or are saved only as they illustrate the revelation of personal torment or transcendence.[5]

I   L'Ombilic des limbes

The initial text in *L'Ombilic des limbes* is a continuation of the ideas presented in *Correspondance avec Jacques Rivière*. Insisting that his texts are intrinsically attached to his life, Artaud proposes to "show his mind" rather than to present any "works." The value of his book is to be judged in relation to reality rather than on literary terms: "Je voudrais faire un Livre qui dérange les hommes, qui soit comme une porte ouverte et qui les mène où ils n'auraient jamais consenti à aller, une porte simplement abouchée avec la réalité" (I, 62).[6] His own reality, the truth of one who has suffered, will change the lives of those who abide by conventional formal standards, for life is not a structure of changeless forms but "de brûler des questions" (I, 61)[7] in the exploration of deeper strata of human experience.

L'Ombilic des limbes is a diverse collection which includes three letters, three poems, four prose texts, a scenario, and a play, as well as the preface. The physical and mental suffering of the writer is the unifying topic, as the preface indicates, and the lyrical or authorial "I" is omnipresent. Even those texts which appear to partake of fictional qualities, such as "Paul les Oiseaux" ("Paul the Birds"), are part of the global enterprise of revealing ill-being. Constantly watching himself, observing his own inability to think deeply, Artaud sees only a series of ruptures which expose inadequate facets of his mental process.

Four prose texts represent physical and mental states in their most immediate sense, as quasiclinical data. Somatic self-perception is an urgent subject in three of these, "Une grande ferveur pensante et surpeuplée . . ." ("A great thinking, overpopulated fervor . . ."), "Description d'un état physique" ("Description of a Physical State"), and "il y a une angoisse acide et troublée . . ." ("There is an acid, troubled anguish . . ."). The body reveals its presence through pain and anguish, and the reality perceived by this altered sensory experience replicates its discontinuity and confusion:

Il faudrait maintenant parler de la décorporisation de la réalité, de cette espèce de rupture appliquée, on dirait, à se multiplier entre les choses et le sentiment qu'elles produisent sur notre esprit, la place qu'elles doivent prendre. (I, 75)[8]

In contrast with Artaud's own battle for a sense of reality, the subject of André Masson's painting described in the fourth prose text, "Un ventre fin . . ." ("A fine belly . . ."), is secure and genuine: "L'esprit est sûr. Il a bien un pied dans ce monde. La grenade, le ventre, les seins, sont comme des preuves attestatoires de la réalité" (I, 77).[9] Masson's painted figure has a more secure grasp of reality than Artaud's organic body. Artaud's model for physical existence is, in this case, taken from a lifeless painting which has a greater vital force than himself. This attraction may be compared with his contrast between the product of poetic composition by others and the process by which he himself creates: in both instances, Artaud fuses logical categories to define an ideal of creativity and existence which is both physical presence and work of art.

The images of anguish in *L'Ombilic des limbes* are those of sensation, and most pervasively, of cold. Ice or ice cubes are highly negative, concrete metaphors for the cessation of thought, perception and life. Artaud is so acutely aware of his corporeal heterogeneity, of the body as an ill-functioning assemblage which fails to achieve any unified direction, that images of separation and diffusion abound. Ice, which dulls sensation and abstracts parts of the body from somatic perception, represents an alien presence within the individual.

In the first letter included in *L'Ombilic des limbes* an elixir is sought which would be able to "exhausser mon abaissement, équilibrer ce qui tombe, réunir ce qui est séparé, recomposer ce qui est détruit" (I, 67).[10] Each effort to attain this unity is a failure, but the diverse stratagems evoked in *L'Ombilic des limbes*—taking drugs, writing poetry, identification with a person who has historical density, creation of a play—are themselves united through the quest to overcome fragmentation. From the outset, Artaud's writing defies efforts at classification and interpretation, yet as it is released into the world, detached from the experience which is its source, it takes on recognizable shapes.

"Le Jet de sang" ("The Spurt of Blood")[11] is one text which lends itself to interpretation and to association with other plays of the early part of this century. Beginning with two young lovers who repeat their contentment with love and the world, the opening scene is interrupted by a cataclysm in which an immense wheel is heard, wind separates the pair, and a profusion of human, animal and manufactured objects falls from the sky. Two new characters, a medieval knight and a wet-nurse with enormous breasts, enter arguing and comment upon the first couple, whom they accuse of incest. The nurse extracts gruyère cheese from her voluminous pockets and flees, while the knight begins to eat the cheese. The young man returns to express a vague, terrible revelation, and an assorted group—priest, cobbler, beadle, procuress, judge, costermonger—appears like shadows. As the young man explains that he has lost his "wife," the priest intervenes to ask which part of her body the young man alluded to most frequently. His reply, "God," so disconcerts the priest that he takes on a Swiss accent.

Night falls suddenly, causing chaos onstage. An immense hand—the hand of God—grasps the procuress by her flaming hair, and she appears naked, then bites God on the wrist. The spurting blood of the title appears, followed by the death of all those onstage except the procuress. The nurse, now flat-chested, returns carrying the young girl, who has died. They are followed by the knight, who demands his cheese; in response, the nurse lifts her skirts. As the young man, transfixed, and the horrified knight look on, scorpions emerge from beneath the nurse's dress and attack the knight, whose sex organ swells and splits. The young man and the procuress flee, and the girl revives with the curtain line: "La vierge! ah, c'était ça qu'il cherchait!" (I, 95).[12]

The complexity of this short play makes it resemble a sketch rather than a complete dramatic text, but it introduces important elements of Artaud's dramaturgy. Objects proliferate and are transformed with no logical source or agent, as is common in Surrealist writing and painting. Even human beings—the nurse and the knight—undergo physical metamorphosis, while death is not an irreversible condition. The theme of incest, suggested between the young couple, will later motivate the action in *Les Cenci* in the more sinister form of paternal assault on a daughter. Mature women are shown to be disgusting because of their association with physical functions such as childbirth, breastfeeding, and copulation. The fever pitch of the play, along with the use of characters as signs and shapes, rather than as fully developed people, point to *Le Théâtre et son double* and foreshadow Artaud's interpretation of Balinese theater.

The same terse, abbreviated style present in "Le Jet de sang" marks "Paul les Oiseaux, ou La Place de l'amour" ("Paul the Birds, or The Place or Love"), but with a significant difference. The gaps in sequence which give the play an abstract, paratactic quality are filled with authorial interventions in "Paul les Oiseaux." Artaud thus has an opportunity to explore the relationship between his perception and his subject—a discontinuity which is emphasized, rather than being effaced, by his discourse. The text is, as the appended letter indicates, a projected scenario which is prefaced by two brief essays that converge on the cinematic subject. In brief, the scenario concerns the painter Paolo Uccello, his wife Selvaggia (who is dying of "hunger"), and two other painters, Brunelleschi and Donatello, who represent carnal and spiritual presences. The psychological struggle between the three men ("car nous sommes *uniquement* dans l'Esprit"[13]) culminates in Brunelleschi's symbolic ejaculation of a large white bird which marks his succumbing to the stress of the situation. Uccello, the central character, is aware of sexual feelings but finds them "chilling"; he is removed from the logical order in which men fight over women. Artaud's inability to identify fully with Uccello and think himself into Uccello's mind is clearly indicated by the first essay, in which he describes himself as being separated from his subject by "mental glass." Discontinuity reigns in the projected set design, which is a complex array of arcades and levels. In every respect, then, the structure of "Paul les Oiseaux" reflects that of Artaud's own fragmented perceptions of himself and the world.

Two other texts with Uccello's name in their titles appear in the first volume of the *Oeuvres complètes*. The first is a different version of the *Ombilic des limbes* scenario under the same title, with an addition, "Prose pour l'homme au crâne de citron" ("Prose for the Man with the Lemon Skull," I, 301–308). The text presents the relationship between Artaud and Uccello somewhat more explicitly: Artaud's desire for self-determination leads him to become the myth and the person of Uccello under the translated name "Paul the Birds" ("Paul les Oiseaux"). The subtitle becomes a question posed to and by Uccello-Artaud: "Où est la place de l'amour?" ("Where is the place / seat of love?" I, 302). For the Uccello figure, who lives entirely in the realm of the mind, there is an answer, albeit an ambiguous one, which "participe au détachement général de l'esprit de Paolo Uccello et le nourrit peut-être un peu en vivant" (I, 305–306).[14] This unstated answer gives him the birth impulse; perhaps it is the desire for self-perpetuation through procreation. The prose text which follows, "Prose pour l'homme au crâne de citron," explains that Artaud writes about himself rather than a given subject. Extolling the freedom of texts situated in the mind, he presents a criterion for the judgment of art: "*Il n'y a qu'une chose qui fasse l'art, la palpabilité des intentions de l'homme. C'es la conscience qui fait la vérité*" (I, 308).[15]

"Uccello le Poil" ("Uccello the Hair," 1926)[16] is a prose text which addresses to Uccello an interpretation of his work as a "myth of hairs"

(I, 170). The gigantic shadow of a single hair reveals to Uccello the infinitely complex realm of perspective, while this same hair marks Uccello's distance from the undifferentiated abyss of madness. The mental geometry generated by this hair leads not only to Uccello's perspective painting, but also to the complex multilevel stage sets which are described in the two scenario sketches.[17]

The poems included in *L'Ombilic des limbes* are the most enigmatic and least satisfying part of the collection. They are a compromise between extant verse form—which Artaud abandoned after these efforts[18]—and the new perceptions which he presents elsewhere in the volume. All three poems superimpose images of the earthy macrocosm and the corporeal microcosm:

> Avec moi dieu-le-chien, et sa langue
> qui comme un trait perce la croûte
> la double calotte en voûte
> de la terre qui le démange
>
> (I, 65)

> Les yeux ragent, les langues tournent
> le ciel afflue dans les narines
>
> (I, 75)

> sur les tables le ciel idole
> s'arc-boute, et le sexe fin
>
> trempe une langue de glace
> dans chaque trou, dans chaque place
> que le ciel laisse en avançant.
>
> (I, 79)[19]

Repeatedly, the integral surface of earth or body is violated by an unpleasant or obscene intrusion, a pattern which becomes even more common Artaud's poetry after 1945. The simultaneous presence of images which are more shocking and more traditional than those of *L'Ombilic des limbes* as a whole gives the impression that in these poems Artaud is literally bursting through even the freest existing verse forms.

II   Le Pèse-nerfs

The varied typography, imagery and tone of *L'Ombilic des limbes* attest to the discontinuity of thought and expression which Artaud revealed to Jacques Rivière. *Le Pèse-nerfs (The Nerve Scale)*, at once more homogeneous and less "literary," is a further step away from subjects outside the self. In a text which begins "Toute écriture est de la cochonnerie" ("All writing is filth"), Artaud announces the defiant significance of the volume's title:

> Et je vous l'ai dit: pas d'oeuvres, pas de langue,
>   pas de parole, rien
> Rien, sinon un beau Pèse-Nerfs
> Une sorte de station incompréhensible et toute droite
>   au milieu de tout dans l'esprit. (I, 121)[20]

Like the dial of a scale, the ideal text would register the variations of the writer's "nervous" state as a direct communication between poet and audience. The reading of this gauge is not to be mistaken for understanding, because no rational approach to the "incomprehensible" nerve scale can succeed.

Le Pèse-nerfs is unusual among Artaud's texts in that the poetic voice is not always that of an isolated individual. He links himself with a movement—Surrealism—and a woman—the actress Génica Athanasiou. Artaud's participation in the Surrealist movement is the subject of a brief allusion in the opening text: for once, he is able to use the first-person plural: "Nous sommes quelques-uns à cette époque à avoir voulu attenter aux choses, créer en nous des espaces à la vie, des espaces qui n'étaient pas dans l'espace" (I, 101).[21] But he cannot personally accomplish this mapping of interior space, much as he approves of it; his mind is eternal virtuality, "an arrested void."

This connection with a group, however tenuous, is more satisfactory than Artaud's relationship with Génica Athanasiou, as it is reflected in the three texts entitled "Lettres de ménage" ("Household Letters"). The subject of these letters is a quarrel over Artaud's use of "a certain substance" (opium), which his correspondent blames for his physical and mental disarray. As in his letter to the legislator of antinarcotics laws (in *L'Ombilic des limbes*), Artaud insists that he alone can judge his need for drugs, and he adds that far from causing his problems, the "substance" assuages them. Apart from this disagreement, Artaud finds other faults in the woman: "Comme toutes les femmes tu juges avec ton sexe, non avec ta pensée" (I, 124);[22] she is more concerned with her own career than with his needs; and she is a psychic illiterate, incapable of understanding his deepest feelings. It should be noted that despite this violently misogynous rhetoric,

Artaud had many women friends, especially in his later years.
Nevertheless, he was never to have a satisfactory intimate relationship with a woman; like his association with the Surrealist movement,
his experiment with domestic life was brief and unsuccessful.

> Tous les termes que je choisis pour penser sont pour moi des TERMES au
> sens propre du mot, de véritables terminaisons, des aboutissements de mes
>   mentales. Je suis vraiment LOCALISE par mes termes. . . . Je suis
> vraiment paralysé par mes termes, par une suite de terminaisons. (I, 116)[23]

The fluctuating state measured by the nerve scale can be contrasted
with the frigid stasis of these endings, which are exemplified in the
quotation by the repetition of the world *terme*. Yet Artaud still hopes
that some day—the period of ten years is mentioned—his vision will
become generalized, his attitude will be vindicated, and his anguished effort will come to an end.

A separate work included at the end of *Le Pèse-nerfs*, "Fragments
d'un journal d'enfer" ("Fragments of a Journal of Hell"), continues the
work of self-definition and self-analysis with one important addition:
the central position of the body is emphasized. In an earlier fragment,
Artaud states that his sole remaining occupation is to remake himself;
now it appears that this activity will be corporeal as well as mental:
"Rien ne me touche, ne m'intéresse que ce qui s'adresse *directement*
à ma chair" (I, 139).[24] Links between life and the mind are multiple, if
problematic; the union of intellect and the subconscious produces a
new life. However, the material quality of life remains subordinate to
the realm of pain and shadow. Physical existence becomes Artaud's
major theme in his later work, just as the body becomes its structure,
but in *Le Pèse-nerfs* his primary concern is the mind. It is a sign of
Artaud's lingering allegiance to Cartesian tradition that he steadfastly
maintains a distinction between the mind and the body.

Several prose texts which date from this period but were not
published in book form[25] also discuss the special relationship of body,
mind, and cosmos for Artaud. "Position de la chair" ("Position of the
Flesh," 1925) is the statement of one who, having lost both physical
and mental wholeness, must reshape an integral life: "Tous les
systèmes que je pourrai édifier n'égaleront jamais mes cris d'homme
occupé à refaire sa vie" (I, 351).[26] His insistence on the fundamental
nature of physical sensation reappears in "Manifeste en langage clair"
("Manifesto in Clear Language") with the explanation that he must
rely on bodily stimuli because his mind fails him.

Some of the images chosen for the self in this period are explicitly those of a dead body. In "Correspondance de la momie" ("The Mummy's Correspondence"), for example, he needs to be reborn after the cocoonlike state of mummification, in which he lacks intellectual density and is immobilized by wrappings. The idea that he is already, if reversibly, dead—which reappears in *L'Art et la mort*—is presented in Artaud's response to the questionnaire of the magazine *Disque vert* on the subject "Is suicide a solution?": "On m'a suicidé, c'est-à-dire. Mais que penseriez-vous d'un suicide antérieur?" (I, 318).[27] Again in "Nouvelle lettre sur moi-même" ("New Letter on Myself"), the mind is a function of the body, where "il entasse une sombre et intraduisible science, pleine de marées souterraines, d'édifices concaves, d'une agitation congelée" (I, 350).[28] Neither sufficient in themselves nor coexisting harmoniously, mind and body corrupt one another, adding to Artaud's anguish.

III   L'Art et la Mort

L'Art et la mort (Art and Death, 1928), the third and last of Artaud's collections of texts from the 1920s, returns to themes which appear in the preceding texts and adds a more explicit preoccupation with death.[29] The volume has the same title as the first text, a lecture which Artaud gave at the Sorbonne on March 22, 1928, under the auspices of the "Philosophical Scientific Group for the Examination of New Tendencies."[30] It is an apprehension of death by the living mind, which sees from the depths of its agony that "la mort n'est pas hors du domaine de l'esprit, qu'elle est dans certaines limites connaissable et approchable par une certaine sensibilité," and that after this experience "tu étais mort et voici que de nouveau tu te retrouves vivant—SEULEMENT CETTE FOIS TU ES SEUL" (I, 151n, 149).[31] The individual consciousness is potentially capable of this perception at four moments: in childhood, in the depths of anguish, in dreams, and under the influence of drugs. Hence death, the ultimate human mystery, can be explored in art through the intermediaries which Artaud himself used.

The second text of *L'Art et la mort* is also mystical in tone and subject matter. This letter to a clairvoyant adds the revelations of a female medium whom Artaud visited with André Breton to drugs and dreams in the inventory of experiences which relieve his fear of death and of the future in general. In the presence of this woman, Artaud finds that his emotions fade, he becomes indifferent, and he abdicates his intelligence. She is, like himself, an exceptional being, and his

outrage at her shabby, contingent life repeats his reaction to his own
state: "Je ne puis me faire à cette idée que vous soyez soumise aux
conditions de l'Espace, du Temps, que les nécessités corporelles
vous pèsent" (I, 159).[32]

Even more mystical is "L'Enclume des Forces" ("The Anvil of
Forces"), a complex vision of the universal absolute revealed by the
fire and flux which emanate from Artaud: "Tous ces reflux commen-
cent à moi. . . . Le monde y bave comme la mer rocheuse, et moi
avec les reflux de l'amour. . . . Il faut que ce feu commence à moi" (I,
175–76). In a fire of tongues, the earth opens like a wounded body,
showing its secrets: "La terre est mère sous la glace du feu" (I, 173);
miraculous generation unites opposites. A conjunction of "the Three
Rays" glows from a center which is made of absolute fire, "la pointe
épouvantable de la force qui se brise dans un tintamarre tout bleu" (I,
174).[33] Above this vision hangs the "Double-Horse," which throws
the earth into shadow. The City, enormous in the play of light and
shadow, arises behind this complex and dynamic vision—a city of
arches and cellars which is inhabited by an enormous body (the
poet's) whose head crawls with dreams. Is "L'Enclume des forces" a
dream text or perhaps a vision under the influence of opium?
Whatever its source, it is a text of unusual strength and mystery; its
cosmic vision reappears in similar terms in the poetic novel
Héliogabale (1934).

The four remaining texts in *L'Art et la mort*[34] are diverse approaches to the problem of human sexuality, a question which
exacerbates Artaud's anguish throughout his adult life. Two pieces,
"Héloïse et Abélard" and "Le Clair Abélard," are projective explorations of the medieval scholar in the manner of Artaud's identifications
with the Uccello "myth." Abelard violated the taboo against fornica-
tion and was castrated. His tragedy poses much the same question as
Uccello's: "where is the place of love?" Certainly, Heloise was a
temptation: an imaginary letter from Abelard to a male friend is a
tissue of surrealist erotic imagery which prepares an unequivocally
sexual vision of Heloise: "Mais c'est qu'Héloïse aussi a des jambes. Le
plus beau c'est qu'elle ait des jambes. Elle a aussi cette chose en
sextant de marine, autour de laquelle toute magie tourne et broute,
cette chose comme un glaive couché" (I, 162).[35] Their love is mental
as well as physical, but the force of God, reviled by Artaud, rises up
and suddenly "THEY" castrate him with scissors. Instantly, Heloise
loses her beauty, for Abelard can no longer desire her. As in

"L'Enclume des forces," all desire begins and ends with the subject, not with the thing desired.

"Le Clair Abélard" ("The Bright Abelard"), while less anecdotal and more personal, is an important text in that it sheds light not only upon Artaud's fascination with castration but also on the sources of his theory of universal cruelty as it evolves toward *Le Théâtre et son double*. Sexual pleasure in so great a man as Abelard has wide-ranging effects: it breaks the historical flow of martyred women, as it loosens the chains of knowledge. His clarity, the brightness of the title, is touched with menace despite its beauty: "Le plaisir fait une tranchante et mystique musique sur le tranchant d'un rêve effilé" (I, 167);[36] one can hear the multilating knife being sharpened. But, as in the Uccello texts, Artaud is observing himself through the vehicle of Abelard, revealing, simultaneously, an unattained cosmic vision:

Pauvre homme! Pauvre Antonin Artaud! C'est bien lui cet impuissant qui escalade les astres, qui s'essaie à confronter sa faiblesse avec les points cardinaux des éléments. . . . S'il pouvait créer autant d'éléments, fournir au moins une métaphysique de désastres, le début serait l'écroulement! (I, 169)[37]

Sexual privation is terrible, a foretaste of death, yet Abelard's punishment has a strong imaginative attraction: Artaud marvels at the beauty contained in the image of a castrato.

The two texts which close *L'Art et la mort* are further explorations of sexuality through the objectivization of Artaud's preoccupations in the expression of other artists. "L'Automate personnel" ("The Personal Automaton"), dedicated to the poet-painter Jean de Boschère, is a reaction to one of his paintings. A descriptive passage is dominated by the threatening figure of a witch and by the obscene "personal automaton," which is outlined against indistinct depths. Although woman appears as a sexually voracious and dangerous creature and the sexual urge is an annoying torment, Artaud renounces neither sex nor heterosexuality. "La Vitre de l'amour" ("The Windowpane of Love") begins with the same emotionally defined couple: an unpleasant, promiscuous woman and a man (the narrative voice) who is forced by his sexual drives to glorify her: "Je la voulais miroitante de fleurs," the text begins, "avec de petits volcans accrochés aux aisselles, et spécialement cette lave en amande amère et qui était au centre de son corps dressé" (I, 183).[38]

Under a brilliant nocturnal sky, he dreams of making love to an unclean scullery maid. He is a student working on a thesis on his eternal subject, "les avortements de l'esprit humain à ces seuils épuisés de l'âme jusqu'où l'esprit de l'homme n'atteint pas" (I, 184).[39] At the moment when he finally decides to speak to her, a group of heads enters through his window, then a gang begins to chase the maid—a gang which includes Hoffmann, Achim von Arnim, and Matthew Lewis, whose novel *The Monk* Artaud later translated. The earth opens and Gérard de Nerval, the largest of them all, appears accompanied by a miniature Artaud. They discuss various oblique approaches to the woman—at this point the text takes on dialogue form—and then leave; following their advice, the student-narrator soon finds the woman in his arms. The names of Heloise and Abelard as well as that of Cleopatra are invoked as indices of the great love they share, but morning brings an evaporation of the vision. Life returns to its usual pattern of impeded thought and obsessions: "Il n'y eût bientôt plus qu'une immense montagne de glace sur laquelle une chevelure blonde pendait" (I, 188).[40]

L'Art et le mort, despite its abstract title, moves beyond the personal, psychological preoccupations of *Le Pèse-nerfs*, *L'Ombilic des limbes*, and the *Correspondance*, but the texts never escape the fundamental situation of Artaud's fragmented and suffering mind. He is willing to write about subjects other than himself, but only as they touch on or reflect his own struggle with language, the mind and the cosmos.

IV   *Artaud and the Surrealists*

A word should be added to the discussion of Artaud's nontheatrical texts of the twenties concerning his writings for and against the Surrealist movement. In early September 1924 Artaud wrote to Mme Toulouse that he had been solicited by those who were then Dadaists to join the embryonic Surrealist movement, and he comments that, while he alone holds the key to surrealism, he is "too surrealist" to join any group. As it turned out, he was right, but in the brief period of his adherence to the movement, he made several interesting contributions to Surrealist reviews.

The letters, the accounts of his activities as director of the Surrealist Research Bureau, and *A la grande nuit ou Le Bluffe surréaliste* (*In Broad Night or The Surrealist Bluff*, 1927) reveal nothing that is not apparent in other texts by Artaud. However, they help to define Artaud's thought more clearly by means of his association with the well-known tenets of Surrealism, and by opposition to them. With terrible precognition, he lambasts current psychiatric theory and practice in "L'Osselet toxique" ("The Toxic Knucklebone," 1928; this text marks his reconciliation with the Surrealists): "Ah, médecine, voici l'homme qui a TOUCHE le danger. Tu as gagné, psychiatrie, tu as GAGNE et il te dépasse" (I, 375). [41] Material success in the world is no match for the physical experience of one who has dared to go beyond the safe province of theory into the dangerous realm of psychic exploration. Other letters contrast the practice of Buddhism with the intellectual and spiritual authority of European universities and the Pope. While Artaud was fascinated with Buddhist belief at this point, his adherence should not be overemphasized in view of his passionate involvement with a variety of non-Western religions as well as his ultimate rejection of all existing cults.

A la grande nuit is at once an attack on Surrealism and a defense of Artaud's own beliefs. Although Breton and Artaud were on close, if wary, terms after a brief period of antagonism, Artaud was bitterly resentful of the Surrealists' attempt to discredit him through politics. The animosity grew after the Surrealists' disruption of the performance of Strindberg's *Dream Play* by Artaud's Alfred Jarry Theater in June 1928. Artaud retorts that Surrealists have no business meddling in politics, for greater topics demand their attention: "Que chaque homme ne veuille rien considérer au delà de sa sensibilité profonde, de son moi intime, voilà pour moi le point de vue de la Révolution intégrale" (I, 365n). [42] Furthermore, the Surrealists are at home in the physical world and love life as much as Artaud scorns it. To Yvonne Allendy, a faithful supporter and the wife of an occultist doctor, he writes that the Surrealists lack any real sense of human or political conditions. [43] Artaud's opposition to orthodox Marxism continues to be an important facet of his Mexican lectures, and he consistently refuses to identify allegiance with any political group.

Despite the quantity and variety of poetry and prose written by Artaud in the 1920s, the focus of his activity was elsewhere. From his arrival in Paris in 1920 through 1935, Artaud was primarily a man of the theater, an actor, set designer, manager, director, playwright, and, most important, a theoretician. Although it is tempting to say that in the theater Artaud found a subject outside the preoccupations with his own mind, body, and the cosmos which pervade his prose and poetry, such is not the case. The same problems recur in his work, just as the personal experience of a malevolent power serves as the foundation of Artaud's Theater of Cruelty.

CHAPTER 3

The Search for a Theater

THE elaboration and realization of Antonin Artaud's theory of theater may be divided into three parts: the Alfred Jarry Theater and texts relating to its performances; the Theater of Cruelty and its theoretical basis as stated in *Le Théâtre et son double* (*Theater and Its Double*, 1938), and postwar texts which were performed or intended for performance.[1] The third phase, although fully representative of Artaud's unique status as "human theater" ("homme-théâtre"), comprises monodramatic or radio performances rather than theatrical entities in the full sense of the earlier texts, and this chapter will therefore be restricted to the first two phases. Artuad's own summary of his work in the theater and the position it takes with regard to other contemporary efforts appears in a lecture presented in Mexico, "Le Théâtre d'après-guerre" ("Postwar Theater," VIII, 209–27).

The question of sources for Artaud's concept of theater is highly problematic in view of his lack of reference to other authors, directors or texts.[2] The Alfred Jarry Theater obviously has some connection with the creator of King Ubu, who was a precursor in the realm of "living theater," but the naming of the company seems to be a generalized homage rather than an indication of specific influence. Artaud had worked with the most innovative directors of his time—Aurélien Lugné-Poë, Louis Jouvet, Charles Dullin—only to reject them explicitly; whether he knew the groundbreaking work of Gordon Craig or Adolphe Appia is uncertain. He was probably familiar with the principles of Jacques Copeau, whose Théâtre du Vieux Colombier inspired several of the directors with whom Artaud collaborated. Another contiguous theory of theater which he knew was that of Nietzsche, but again, any assertion of influence is subject to qualifications so serious as to place it in doubt. Artaud's originality may not be as great as his own statements imply, for the contemporary work in the theater certainly must have come to his attention.

I *The Alfred Jarry Theater*

As early as 1924, Artaud wrote his first theatrical manifesto, "L'Evolution du décor" ("The Evolution of Set Decoration").[3] The title is deceptive, for he sees theater primarily as an interior experience; the external appearance of the set matters only insofar as it reflects a psychic model. True theater, then, exists in two "places": in the mind and in life, that is, in the cosmic life which is a "transsubstantiation de la vie" (II, 12).[4] The director communicates with the author by a mystical magnetism that leads him to convey the spirit rather than the letter of the text.

Even at this early date, then, Artaud is exploring ways to go beyond the written word. Communion between director and author is only possible when the director himself attains a high level of consciousness by freeing himself of everyday preoccupations. The audience in turn becomes part of the interpenetration of minds and partakes of the "divine terror" of the theater. As for the production itself, Artaud demands that it be intellectualized and alludes to the exemplary activity of clowns, but he does not elaborate on these concepts. The major points in this text—global consideration of theater in its relationship with reality, combined with a lack of pragmatic information—reappear throughout Artaud's essays on theater for the next fifteen years.

The launching of the Alfred Jarry Theater was accompanied by a number of texts which publicized and defined the productions. Although Artaud collaborated in this venture with Roger Vitrac and Robert Aron, the explanatory texts are by Artaud, with only token guidance and ultimate approval from Vitrac and Aron.[5] The inevitable conflict between Artaud's hostility to pragmatism and the financial and logistical realities of theatrical productions caused several problems. The statements of principles vacillate, often taking an aggressively self-defensive stance. When the Alfred Jarry Theater failed, Artaud's desire for a theatrical forum of his own was intensified. Nevertheless, his first independent theater is significant for two reasons: first, it provided Artaud with an early opportunity to formulate and implement his theatrical concepts, and second, its failure spurred him on toward the Theater of Cruelty.

In his first announcement of the Alfred Jarry Theater, Artaud deplores the reduction of theater to a superfluous "play" and calls for a revitalization of the "true operation" of the stage. His theater is as painful and as effective as a visit to a surgeon or a dentist; the spectator

"doit être bien persuadé que nous sommes capables de le faire crier"
(III, 22). [6] Further principles emerge in the publicity brochure for the
1926–27 season: the performance is to have the appearance of being
unique, as incapable of repetition as any other important human
action, [7] and it is to implicate the mind, the senses, the flesh, even the
destiny of the audience. Success is postulated on a "miracle of
chance" which will lead the audience to reject the customary version
of reality and adhere to Artaud's outlook. The text is the one
"invulnerable" element of the production, not as words but "simplement quant au déplacement d'air que son énonciation provoque" (II,
26). [8]

The "Manifeste pour un théâtre avorté" ("Manifesto for an
Aborted Theater," 1926), which takes its title from the apparent
failure of the enterprise, repeats these principles with increasing
emphasis on the metaphysical qualities of performance. A postscript
obliquely denounces the Surrealists' objection to theater as counter-
revolutionary: Artaud insists that only through a theater which effects
the whole human entity, not merely living conditions, can a true
Revolution be accomplished. Defiant in defeat, Artaud adds:

Il est certain que si j'avais fait un théâtre, ce que j'aurais fait se serait aussi peu
apparenté à ce que l'on a l'habitude d'appeler le théâtre que la représentation d'une obscénité quelconque ressemble à un ancien mystère religieux.
(II, 33)[9]

The "obscenity" is, of course, existing theater, while the ancient
religious mystery is Artaud's own.

The announcement for the second season of the Alfred Jarry
Theater reaffirms an antiillusory, antirepetitive stance. The repertoire is to be chosen from texts which are timeless in their exploration
of human anguish, revolt and aspiration. Along with Vitrac's *Victor,
ou Les Enfants au pouvoir (Victor, or Power to the Children)* and
Cyril Tourneur's Elizabethan *Revenger's Tragedy*, this flier projects a
collaborative "manifesto-play" which is to incorporate the broadest
possible range of staging techniques. Beginning with the statement
that theater is not an end but a means, Artaud reaffirms that the
Alfred Jarry Theater will make theater serve his own ends, not serve
the cause of other theaters. The earlier plea for an "invulnerable" text
is now abandoned; now Artaud states that the group respects neither
author nor text; rather, it will choose plays with regard to substantive
meaning—the dogma of the Alfred Jarry Theater—and not for their

prestige. A 1929 circular uses the terms "spectacle total" and "spectacle intégral" to describe the goal of the company and looks forward to the production of Jarry's *Ubu Roi* and one of Vitrac's plays which was later known as *Le Coup de Trafalgar (The Trafalgar Coup)*. Artaud persists in believing that a theater which fully realizes its own potential can transform the world.

Le Théâtre Alfred Jarry et l'hostilité publique (The Alfred Jarry Theater and Public Hostility), a 1930 brochure, summarizes and justifies the efforts made by Artaud and Vitrac over four busy and frustrating years. Although it was not written as an obituary, it did, in fact, coincide with the end of the project and Artaud's quarrel with Vitrac. The brochure consists of a declaration of principles, photographic montages from Artaud's pantomime, "La Pierre philosophale" ("The Philosopher's Stone," following II, 64, text II, 96–106), an extensive series of excerpts from criticism of performances by the Alfred Jarry Theater, and letters concerning the company's troubles with the controversial production of Strindberg's *Dream Play* and the unauthorized performance of Act III of Claudel's *Partage de midi*.[10]

Despite the controversy surrounding the Alfred Jarry Theater, the company's goal remained unchanged: "Par des *moyens spécifiquement théâtraux* de contribuer à la ruine du théâtre tel qu'il existe actuellement en France" (II, 51).[11] When conventional theater collapses, it will take with it all the literary and ideological underpinning implied by its existence. Public hostility to experimental theater appears in nine forms which range from the lack of capital to adverse journalistic criticism. Artaud is not entirely unpragmatic: under the heading "Position of the Alfred Jarry Theater," he states that the customary indices of success—presumably, the number of people attending performances—will not be neglected. The key to success is *actuality* and the most powerful tool is a humor which leads to "Absolute laughter." Further objectives include the use of eroticism to overcome repression without recourse to the unconscious and a theater which takes place on an open, human level without hidden allusions or secret structures. The vexing question of sources for the Alfred Jarry Theater is partially resolved when the brochure lists the elements of a "new tradition": structures furnished by Chinese, Black American and Soviet theaters are to be infused with the spirit of humor found in Jarry and the rigorous method of Raymond Roussel (II, 61).

The section on staging is closer to Artaud's ideas in later theoretical texts. Characters are to be played as stereotypes, each with a distinct voice. The projection of a new form of pantomime looks forward to the "sign language" discussed later in *Le Théâtre et son double;* the call for exploitation of technical, verbal, and gestural means in order to inspire strong audience reactions suggests the staging of *Les Cenci,* which was five years in the future.

Among the texts which follow the expository material in the 1930 brochure, two are critical pastiches in conversational form; the second, which concerns Vitrac's *Victor,* is especially noteworthy because it includes dialogue attributed to Father Ubu, Vitrac, and Artaud.[12] While the "critics" discuss the character of Ida Mortemart (a beautiful woman afflicted with gas), Ubu makes insulting or threatening remarks, and he finally reveals himself as André Breton by using Breton's published comments from the Second Surrealist Manifesto. If *Ubu Roi* is accepted as a masterpiece, Artaud argues that *Victor* and Roussel's theater in general should also be acclaimed. The character Ida Mortemart is also the subject of a letter inserted in the program for *Victor:* the reader is reminded of Artaud's fundamental quarrel with the world while he is seated in the theater. This letter finds that Ida's repellent affliction represented the filth in a fallen mankind, an indication of human duality:

Il [Vitrac] a voulu épuiser le côté tremblant et qui s'effrite, non seulement du sentiment, mais aussi de la pensée humaine, mettre au jour l'antithèse profonde et éternelle entre l'asservissement de notre état et de nos fonctions matérielles et notre qualité d'anges et de purs esprits. (II, 44)[13]

The basic problem of Artaud's being in the world remains in the forefront despite his other preoccupations.

II *Artaud the Playwright*

While the texts connected with the Alfred Jarry Theater have received some public exposure, Artaud's other theatrical writings from this period are virtually unknown. For example, an early dramatic text, *Samourai, ou Le Drame du sentiment (Samurai, or The Drama of Sentiment,* 1923–25), indicates a phase in the evolution of Artaud's theater under the influence of both Japanese theater[14] and Strindberg and contains, as well, embryonic elements of Artaud's later theatrical practice.

In *Samourai,* the tormented protagonist passes from attraction to his mother, the Queen, to his sister, and finally, after killing his father, to a female servant.[15] Masked figures are not as unexpected in the Japanese context as they are later in Artaud's staging of Vitrac's plays, but the masks to be used in *Samourai* are unconventional in size and appearance, not unlike those used by Jarry in *Ubu Roi*. Even the protagonist is masked throughout the play: he appears as an old man, but in the final tableau he is revealed to be young. The use of a doll as a property of symbolic value—the Samourai says that it represents the broken, larval state to which his dream is reduced— recurs in "La Pierre philosophale," another early dramatic text. While neither masks nor dolls are novel, the text displays a more important characteristic: the dominance of violent, startling action over the spoken text. The speeches reveal the hidden fears and desires which determine the course of the play's development, rather than being recognizable as conversation, while stage events are gestural and highly kinetic. Although *Samourai* is an imperfect, unfinished text, it indicates continuity between Artaud's experience as actor and poet (which characterized his activity at the time of its composition) and his desire for a more complete involvement with the theater.

Only one play by Artaud was actually performed by the Alfred Jarry Theater. *Ventre brûlé, ou La Mère folle (Burned Belly, or The Mad Mother)* opened the first series of performances, but the text has unfortunately been lost.[16] Although the pantomime "La Pierre philosophale" appears in the form of photo-montages in "Le Théâtre Alfred Jarry et l'hostilité publique," it was never performed in public; the interesting "argument for the stage" entitled "Il n'y a plus de firmament" ("The Firmament is No More"), which probably dates from 1931, is incomplete and was never staged.

The characters in "La Pierre philosophale" are Doctor Pale, his wife Isabelle, and Harlequin, who has fallen in love with Isabelle and volunteers for one of the doctor's experiments. Pale is looking for the philosopher's stone, but his experiment consists of cutting off Harlequin's arms and legs. While the doctor's back is turned, Isabelle and Harlequin make love; they are surprised by Pale and the child just conceived emerges from Isabelle's skirts to reveal itself as a miniature reproduction of Doctor Pale. The character of Harlequin is double; he appears to be a handsome young man; his capacity to regenerate lost limbs makes him monstrous. Harlequin announces that the philosopher's stone will be taken out of his body, like the child from

Isabelle's; although his heterosexuality is emphasized, he also plays a female role.[17] Despite the subtitle "pantomime," this text includes some dialogue to be uttered in a calculated, unnatural manner.

"Il n'y a plus de firmament," like the preceding text and "Le Jet de sang," has a technically ambitious quality. A fragmentary text which follows suggests that Artaud actually planned an outdoor performance in the street. In this script, the appearance of a cosmic cataclysm (the disappearance of the heavens) is followed by a revolutionary uprising led by the "Grand Flaireur" ("Great Sniffer"). A scientific breakthrough, communication with the star Sirius, is debated by ridiculous scientists in the "Fourth Movement" of the play, amid predictions of the end of the world. The cosmic subject of the text reflects Artaud's continuing metaphysical stance, but it is also noteworthy that he is writing about those material conditions of life which he accused the Surrealists of overemphasizing. For example, he suggests that a barter system would alleviate the problem caused by the universal obsession with money. Artaud is not devoid of a social conscience, but it always takes second place to his understanding of the universe.

Finally, the lost play entitled "La Supplice de Tantale" ("The Torture of Tantalus," 1932) was an adaptation of Seneca's *Atreus and Thyestes*, which Artaud hoped to present in Marseilles. The three surviving notes concerning this play suggest that Artaud was already formulating in script form some of the new ideas he had presented in his essays on Balinese theater and in the essay entitled "Le Théâtre et la métaphysique," which later appeared in *Le Théâtre et son double*. The play would be "les paroxysmes d'une action matérielle violente" in order to awaken the audience's sensibility to cosmic evil. Notes on the play also point to this goal: "Pas de libre arbitre. Classifier le Mal. Comprendre son Destin. L'homme, jouet de dieu, Jouet de lui-même" (II, 207).[18]

In the summer of 1931, Artaud attended a performance by a Balinese theatrical troupe which served as a catalyst for his thinking about theater. Constantly struggling with verbal expression, Artaud was struck by the Balinese use of gestures rather than spoken language. Like language, the use of a system of gestures implies a code which can be broken only by the initiated, but for Artaud, the code of Balinese sign-language exists on a higher level than that of words. Furthermore, when theater as language is a system of signs, the director becomes the author, for there is no written dialogue. In addition to gestures, costumes, makeup, properties, and set decorations attain the status of signs in the theatrical language as part of a coherent whole.

Artaud's exposure to Balinese theater coincides with his increasing interest in non-Western religious and philosophical thought and with the influence of René Guénon. His search for a civic celebration which is at once religious in spirit and profane in that it is not linked with a specific cult is answered in the potential of this theater of signs. The ideal of a theater of unsurpassed magnitude remains with Artaud throughout his work toward the Theater of Cruelty.

III   The Theater and Its Double: *A Metaphysical Theater*

The collection of articles, lectures, and notes published by Gallimard in 1938 as *Le Théâtre et son double* is the best known and most influential of Artaud's writings. Besides explaining the premises of the Theatre of Cruelty, these texts reveal the sources and evolution of Artaud's thought in the 1930s. The texts cover five years of composition, and publication was further delayed until after Artaud's trips to Mexico and Ireland; when the volume finally appeared, he was in the asylum at Ville-Evrard.

The first principle of theater proposed in *Le Théâtre et son double* is that it must reflect unity with true culture, an immanence of the metaphysical in the topical. "Culture," one of Artaud's continuing preoccupations, must coincide with cosmic life through the urgency of human desires. In order to unify form and content, signs and the things or ideas they represent, the forms must grow spontaneously out of life, as it is experienced in its truest and most familiar essence:

Briser le langage pour toucher la vie, c'est faire ou refaire le théâtre; et l'important est de ne pas croire que acte doive demeurer sacré, c'est-à-dire réservé. Mais l'important est de croire que n'importe qui ne peut pas le faire, et qu'il y faut une préparation. (IV, 18)[19]

As Artaud explains to Jean Paulhan in a letter written in Havana on January 25, 1936, the "double" of his title is "true life," the creative-destructive energy which is expressed in true theater: "Et par ce double j'entends le grand agent magique dont le théâtre par ses formes n'est que la figuration en attendant qu'il en devienne la transfiguration" (V, 272–73).[20] Theater also has other doubles — the plague, cruelty, and alchemy — but they conjoin in the consummate double which is Life. Artaud finds manifestations of doubles in the Balinese theater, where costumes and gestures spring from implicit metaphysical sources, while his notes for the staging of Strindberg's *Ghost Sonata* propose an explicit use of mannequins as visible doubles for the actors. Existing at the level of "vertical reality," the double is not illusion but the limit of the coincidence of life with the material, a highly volatile state which threatens the everyday activities of humanity with the eruption of hidden forces destined to annihilate the world as we know it.

The greater life of the cosmos which Artaud proposes to "double" in the Theater of Cruelty is dangerous, violent, and evil. Believing that the ultimate descent of cosmic cruelty into the world was imminent and that his idea of theater would assuredly become reality, Artaud was willing to give years of frustrating effort to the cause:

Il s'agit maintenant de savoir si, à Paris, avant les cataclysmes qui s'annoncent, on pourra trouver assez de moyens de réalisation, financiers ou autres, pour permettre à un semblable théâtre de vivre, et celui-ci tiendra de toute façon, parce qu'il est l'avenir. Ou s'il faudra un peu de vrai sang, tout de suite, pour manifester cette cruauté. (IV, 105)[21]

In view of his absolute faith in the enterprise, Artaud's theoretical speculations take on an immediacy which links them with his metaphysics. Although his projected productions, and especially *Les Cenci*, contain violence and bloodshed, this mere physical cruelty is not the true meaning of "cruelty" for Artaud.[22] On the human scale, cruelty is a consciousness which illuminates life in a display of its essential carnage; it is an intellectual rigor which reproduces cosmic determinism, "une sorte d'aride pureté morale qui ne craint pas de payer la vie le prix qu'il faut la payer" (IV, 146).[23] Finding life inexorably cruel, Artaud borrows the gnostic idea of the life-whirlwind, which is an evil so implacable that to combat it by doing good is itself a cruel struggle. Although modern Western literature has lost touch with the forces of cruelty, their influence may be found in tales from other times and other cultures:

Et c'est ainsi que tous les grands Mythes sont noirs et qu'on ne peut imaginer hors d'une atmosphère de carnage, de torture, de sang versé, toutes les magnifiques Fables qui racontent aux foules le premier partage sexuel et le premier carnage d'essences qui apparaissent dans la création. (IV, 38)[24]

Cruelty is life, a necessity, and the theater which proposes to be its double must be a self-perpetuating phenomenon which changes constantly: "Nous ne sommes pas libres. Et le ciel peut encore nous tomber sur la tête. Et le théâtre est fait pour nous apprendre d'abord cela" (IV, 95).[25]

IV *Two Metaphorical Doubles: Plague and Alchemy*

"Le Théâtre et la peste" ("Theater and the Plague"), the first essay in *Le Théâtre et son double,* represents Artaud's most eloquent defense of his theater. Taking the stance of an anti-Augustine, he cites *The City of God* in support of his equation of plague, which kills without destroying the human organs, and theater, which transforms the mind of the populace without killing. While Augustine uses this argument to propose a ban on the theater, Artaud finds that the similarity supports the very goals of his Theater of Cruelty. Drawing on historical accounts of the plague in Cagliari and Marseilles and attributing it to causes more occult than *pasteurella pestis,* he describes the action of the plague as a rapid effacement of the mask of civilization which reveals human potential beyond the deceits of ordinary life. In the theater, as in the plague, humanity confronts its destiny in a unique opportunity to match its own cruelty to that of the universe.

Artaud's second metaphorical double, alchemy, is identified with theater through two conjunctions: their mutual origin in "le drame essentiel" ("the essential drama," i.e., of essences) and the use of theatrical imagery in alchemical language. Both belong to that aspect of creation which, like the "double," involves the material and the ideal, while suggesting the first level, that of essences, by their "vertical reality." The goal of alchemy is to regain this primary realm at the fleeting, vibrating limit of its own being—a goal shared by the Orphic and Eleusinian mysteries on which Artaud bases his theatrical project. More than a decade later, Artaud rejects alchemy in his "Lettre sur *Les Chimères*" (XI, 184–201) because it never reaches this common goal, while true poetry (in this instance that of Gérard de Nerval) confronts the essential danger even at the cost of the poet's life. Even in *Le Théâtre et son double,* references to alchemy are more rhetorical and less urgent than those to the plague.

A third, less complete avatar of the essential drama is found in a few paintings which capture the spasmodic movement of human confrontation with cosmic cruelty. In "La Mise-en-scène et la métaphysique" ("Staging and Metaphysics"), Artaud uses Lucas Van Leyden's *Lot's Daughters* to exemplify the ideographical language or "poetry for the senses" which he will exteriorize on the stage. Poetry in the strongest

sense—valid only insofar as it is metaphysical—goes beyond language: hence, while "poetic," the theater advocated is more closely
related to the paintings of Van Leyden, Grünewald, and Bosch than
to dramatic poetry in the manner of a Racine.

V   Theater as a Language of Signs

Although the mechanics of theatrical production are to derive from
and reflect the metaphysical grounding of Artaud's theory, they take
second place. Yet, because of their inferior status, they must be all
the more carefully regulated. Artaud's forceful conclusion to the
Preface of Le Théâtre et son double is vulnerable to misinterpretation
because it seems to suggest that spontaneous action is sufficient:

Et s'il est encore quelque chose d'infernal et de véritablement maudit dans ce
temps, c'est de s'attarder artistiquement sur des formes, au lieu d'être
comme des suppliciés que l'on brûle et qui font des signes sur leurs bûchers.
(IV, 18)[26]

The creation of a theater conducive to the natural expression of truth
requires artisanal as well as "artistic" work. In the third of Artaud's
letters on language to Jean Paulhan, Artaud notes that he avoids
giving the kind of detailed information which would allow other
directors to duplicate his style: "Je pose des principes rigoureux,
inattendus, d'aspect rébarbatif et terrible, et au moment où l'on
s'attend à me voir les justifier je passe au principe suivant" (IV,
137).[27]

Artaud's lifelong aversion to conventionally clear ideas leads us to
expect little in the way of concrete information from Le Théâtre et son
double. He returns continually to two major stumbling blocks in
Western theater—language and the written text—to the virtual
exclusion of other elements of staging. At the end of "La Mise-en-
scène et la métaphysique," for example, he states that he will avoid an
overlong discussion of all theatrical means of expression by giving
"two or three examples," and then he gives only one: spoken language, which he has already discussed in other contexts. This vague-
ness, as well as concealing techniques from other directors, derives
from the fact that the impact of the essays is more important to Artaud
than their information.

In the first manifesto of the Theater of Cruelty, language and the
dramatic text are integrated with such diverse theatrical resources as
lighting, music, costume, and theatrical architecture in order to give

the reader some insight into Artaud's intentions. Even this coalescence is, of course, deceptive, for only on the stage can the full import of Artaud's principles be realized.

The most important point in this manifesto concerns the visual language—an alphabet of signs—which complements an expanded audible language of noise, music, and screams, as well as words, in the Theater of Cruelty. Words are used inadequately in Western theater and lose their metaphysical dimensions when they are fixed in endlessly repeated masterpieces reserved for an elite audience. For Artaud, those theatrical techniques which have an ephemeral existence in space and time, such as lighting and gestures, have been neglected in favor of the apparent permanence of the written text. Yet, it is these overlooked aspects of theatrical production which have the greatest inherent appeal to the most profound reaches of the human organism and which create a spectacle capable of action on the total being through the senses: "C'est par la peau qu'on fera rentrer la métaphysique dans les esprits" (IV, 118). However, language is not to be abolished: "Ce que le théâtre peut encore arracher à la parole, ce sont ses possibilités d'expansion hors des mots, de développement dans l'espace, d'action dissociatrice et vibratoire sur la sensibilité" (IV, 107).[28] Theater is an organic function like any other, brief and unique. Thus Artaud denies the traditional link between repetition and theater.

In Artaud's view, the director, not the author, makes the most important contribution to this production; ideally, they should be the same person, the spectacle being created by the director in the period of time traditionally allotted to rehearsals. The production would be so minutely regulated by the director that no improvisation by the actors could interfere with his intentions. In fact, Artaud later complained that the failure of *Les Cenci* was due in part to the unwillingness of the actors to accept his complete control. This first manifesto incorporates twenty-one aspects of theatrical performance, but there is no listing for the director: he is the single creator, just as staging is the basis for all theatrical creation, and he holds the key to the sign language which integrates all the elements of production: "Le spectacle sera chiffré d'un bout à l'autre, comme un langage" (IV, 118).[29]

The very breathing of the actors, a topic discussed in "Un Athlétisme affectif" ("An Affective Athleticism"), is part of the code, as are facial expressions, intonation, and the symbolic use of gestures. The influence of the elaborate code of movement in Balinese theater is obvious here. Artaud's own acting style, which was occasionally criticized as being unnatural, was based on the primary consideration of gesture.

Apart from the extreme demands made of a single individual, two other problems arise with regard to Artaud's approach to staging. The first and most frustrating problem for Artaud concerns the public, and in the next-to-last statement in the first manifesto he declares that the theater must exist before the public can even come into being. Artaud's long struggle to establish his theater and its ultimate failure suggest that in the everyday world the reverse is true, for, barring the availability of resources such as those accessible to the producers of a Hollywood spectacle, theater is incapable of creating its own public. At one time Artaud hoped to accomplish a mass extravaganza in a warehouse or even in the street, but, because of the perpetual lack of financial support, he had to be satisfied with a conventional theater. Having failed to find adequate patronage to allow the realization of the Theater of Cruelty in its full scope, Artaud faced the even more galling disappointment of failure to attract an audience sufficient to keep *Les Cenci* open for more than seventeen performances.

The second problem is the choice of subject matter. Artaud's propositions, other than "La Conquête du Mexique" ("The Conquest of Mexico"), are a remarkably mixed group. Two of the titles listed in the first manifesto are part of projects which Artaud hoped to bring to fruition in the early 1930s: the first was an adaptation of *Arden of Feversham*[30] (a work falsely attributed to Shakespeare, it was to have been adapted by André Gide), while the second was Georg Büchner's *Woyzeck*, which, in cooperation with Louis Jouvet, was to illustrate the potential as well as the weakness of the written text. Other proposed subjects in the first manifesto range from Elizabethan works stripped of their texts through the story of Bluebeard, a Sade tale ("Le Chateau de Valmont"), *The Taking of Jerusalem*, the story of Rabbi Simeon from the Zohar, to the Romantic melodramas from which he would choose *Les Cenci*.

Even this list—to which could be added Tourneur's *Revenger's Tragedy* and the adaptation of *Atreus and Thyestes*—provides ample material for several seasons and a stringent test of any director's powers. Although the Elizabethan and Romantic plays might lend themselves less to the manifestation of cruelty than the other works, they do share with Sade and "Bluebeard" the violation of sexual taboos, violent emotion, bloodshed, and a certain dramatic looseness which would allow the director a great deal of freedom. While Artaud's insistence on "destruction-humor" (IV, 108) may find little place in this program, its unlikely presence in the midst of the violence and incest in *Les Cenci* suggests that Artaud could integrate the dramatic quality of humor into even this repertoire.

VI The Project for Totality: "La Conquête du Mexique"

The second manifesto of the Theater of Cruelty abandons the elaborate program of the first in favor of a single project, "La Conquête du Mexique" ("The Conquest of Mexico"). This text has a topical and timeless appeal in its treatment of the tragic fall of Montezuma, the panoply of Aztec culture, and the urgent problems of colonalism and racism. The giant spectacle is to be presented according to the principles of cruelty and to return to the theater "une vie passionée et convulsive" through "rigueur violente [et] condensation extrême des éléments scéniques" (IV, 146).[31] In content, it is to satisfy the requirement that theater recover the relevance of cosmic myths for modern life, and to present conflicts between races, heroes, and superhuman forces. Formally, the manifestation of primeval conflicts is to take place on the level of spectacle rather than that of language, with an acute consciousness of all the dimensions of theatrical space.

Spectator and spectacle would be carefully encoded through the resources of magical incantation:

Si, dans le théâtre digestif d'aujourd'hui, les nerfs, c'est-à-dire une certaine sensibilité physiologique, sont laissés délibérément de côté, livrés à l'anarchie individuelle du spectateur, le Théâtre de la Cruauté compte en revenir à tous les vieux moyens éprouvés de gagner la sensibilité. (IV, 150)[32]

Artaud's fascination with Mexico, which inspired his long visit in 1936, is evident in his projected dramatic denunciation of colonial tyranny, Christianity, and the white culture in general. In its place, he dramatizes the harmony of an Indian culture in which sacred cruelty is reflected in every part of society, from the ritual dances which he proposes to stage to the premonitory dreams of Montezuma.

"Le Théâtre et les dieux" ("Theater and the Gods"), one of the lectures Artaud gave at the National University of Mexico, reinforces the idea that Mexican deities have a privileged relationship with his

CARNEGIE LIBRARY
LIVINGSTONE COLLEGE
SALISBURY, N. C

idea of cruelty. In addition to their bloodthirsty ways, they exist
primarily in space; their mythology is a science of space which closely
resembles theater itself:

Il y a un mouvement aujourd'hui pour séparer le théâtre d'avec tout ce qui
n'est pas l'espace, et pour renvoyer le langage du texte dans les livres d'où il
n'aurait pas dû sortir. Et ce langage de l'espace à son tour agit sur la sensibilité
nerveuse, il fait mûrir le paysage déployé au-dessous de lui. (VIII, 203)[33]

However sympathetic Mexican ideas might be to Artaud, such a vast
spectacle as "La Conquête du Mexique" would require the prover-
bial cast of thousands and substantial funding, but in those economi-
cally depressed years, production on such a lavish scale proved to be
impossible. On January 6, 1934, Artaud gave a dramatic reading at
the home of Lise and Paul Deharme to an audience of prospective
patrons.[34] The promised thirty thousand francs failed to materialize,
and he was finally forced to abandon hope of staging "La Conquête du
Mexique."

VII   *The Project Realized:* Les Cenci

When he chose *Les Cenci* for the debut of the Theater of Cruelty,
Artaud was aware that neither of the works of the same title—a play
by Shelley and a short story by Stendhal—suggests an adaptation
which would be pure theater of cruelty. For Artaud, *Les Cenci*
reveals the exemplary amorality of nature and provides the
framework for a metaphysical attack on the family and society in
general. Artaud believed that the intensity of this drama of incest,
revenge, and parricide, and not the text, would appeal to an audience. Within this somewhat limited scope, the Theater of Cruelty
finally appeared. Despite its ostensible failure, Artaud ultimately
judged it "un succès dans l'Absolu" (VIII, 114).[35]

Les Cenci is the historically based account of a tyrannical father
whose outrageous behavior toward his family—murder of sons and
rape of a daughter—finally moves them to have him murdered; the
assassins drive nails through his head. Against a backdrop of Roman
baroque dynamism and papal intrigue, Cenci's horrible actions are
elevated to a superhuman plane. Time and again he identifies himself
with the implacable force of destiny, with a God as cruel as himself.
Consequently, cruelty is present in both the usual sense of the word
(although the rape and murder occur offstage) and in the special

meaning of the Theater of Cruelty. The family, society, wealth, conventional justice, and the church are also attacked in the highly violent context of the play, for Cenci is rich and powerful, and the setting in sixteenth-century Rome is infiltrated by treacherous churchmen.

Beatrice, Cenci's violated daughter, is a character of unusual power. Although she is a sympathetic clairvoyant and the instigator of the murder plot, her effort to avenge herself is a deed no less terrible than her father's. Once "polluted" by Cenci, she loses her mystical innocence, and her denial of guilt for the patricide to which she confesses reveals an amorality equal to that of the villain. She cries in the closing lines of the play, from the wheel on which she is hung by her hair, "J'ai peur que la mort ne m'apprenne/que j'ai fini par lui ressembler" (IV, 271).[36] The lyric beauty of her speeches, especially in the fifth act when she faces death, is accompanied by her extraordinary appearance on stage, hanging by the hair from the torturer's wheel; although Iya Abdy, the actress who played Beatrice, rejected the actual hanging, the photographs of this scene (V, iii) remain the most vivid illustrations of Artaud's staging.

Compared with Shelley's 1819 text, Artaud's play relies less on spoken language, especially in Act IV, Scene 2, when a plot to assassinate Cenci as he crosses a bridge is enacted rather than narrated. This scene further illustrates Artaud's dictum that words should have the importance they acquire in dreams (IV, 112): in the midst of a violent storm, voices cry out rhythmically, "Cenci, Cenci, Cenci, Cenci," and finally force the Count to respond, precipitating the assassination attempt.

Sound-effects participate in Artaud's language of signs, for it appeals to all the senses, as well as to the mind. In *Les Cenci,* the noise of church bells and factories was recorded and coordinated by Frédéric Désormière with Martenot waves; recorded thunder and crowd noises create a frequently deafening audible counterpart to the terrible visual spectacle. The highly praised set design by Balthus, with its eye-catching staircases, apertures, and machines, carries out Artaud's desire to create an awareness of the many dimensions of scenic space. These two successful aspects of the production, while they puzzled critics, have the effect of exploding the traditional stage-cube with audible and visual allusions to a mysterious and threatening cosmic context which appears in the representative fragment on stage.

VIII *Theater Beyond the Stage*

While Artaud continued to organize theatrical enterprises long after the failure of *Les Cenci*, he also carried his idea of theater with its metaphysical implications into his new project in Mexico. His lectures in Mexico centered on the subject of theater; his poetic performances for French radio in 1947–48 were dramatic events; even when virtually on his deathbed, he still hoped to reconstitute the Theater of Cruelty.

One aspect of Artaud's theater which sharply divides him from the traditional concept of the genre is his hatred of repetition:

> reconnaissons que ce qui a été dit n'est plus à dire; qu'une expression ne vaut pas deux fois, ne vit pas deux fois; que toute parole prononcée est morte et n'agit qu'au moment où elle est prononcée, qu'une forme employée ne sert plus et n'invite qu'à en rechercher une autre, et que le théâtre est le seul endroit au monde où un geste fait ne se recommence deux fois. (IV, 91)[37]

According to Jacques Derrida, Artaud rejects the accumulated sameness which creates a static Being in favor of a theater of "difference," which expends pure presence wildly, without the economizing intermediaries of mimesis or representation.[38] Despite the fact that Artaud's vision denies the essence of traditional theater, which, like ritual behavior, is created to be repeated, it must be understood that in his world the word *theater* includes a unified corpus of audience, actor, and spectacle. This entity breathes, feels cruelty, and finally enacts cruelty as if the three separate elements were one being, and the experience can never be repeated. Like the coming of the Messiah, such a miraculous event would change the minds, if not the lives (Artaud is ambiguous on this point) of all those it touched by revealing a new cosmic order. It is at this asymptotic moment that Theater and Life would become a mobile unity which marks the end of the old, dead world and its population of cadavers.

Artaud's theater and the situation in which he attempted to realize it failed to coincide. Rather than continue the agonizingly fruitless effort to create a new culture in French society by means of the theater, he sought preexisting manifestations of a culture which unites art, religion, and daily life. In the reign of Heliogabalus, the Cabbala, the Tibetan Book of the Dead, other occult texts, and, most important, in the native culture of Mexico, he sought and at times discovered the principles he tried to actualize in the Theater of Cruelty.

CHAPTER 4

Occult Explorations

ARTAUD rejects Western European culture in general because of its reliance on fixed texts, its debased sexuality, and false distinction between the sacred and daily experience. He seeks to replace it with "une culture basée sur l'esprit en relation avec les organes" (VIII, 201),[1] a culture which exists, like theater, in space, infused with a metaphysical life that cannot be fixed in written forms. In such a culture, the mind moves constantly:

Du vide vers les formes, et des formes rentre dans le vide, dans le vide comme dans la mort. Etre cultivé, c'est brûler des formes, brûler des formes pour gagner la vie. C'est apprendre à se tenir droit dans le mouvement incessant des formes qu'on détruit successivement. (VIII, 202)[2]

The static distinction between forms and the void would be replaced by an interpenetration of these two elements through the agency of fire, and life within the forms is revealed in their burning. For Artaud, however, the cultivated individual remains inviolate in the configuration; he would be the single constant in a world of dynamism. The imagery which Artaud chooses for this description recalls the martyr on the stake of *Le Théâtre et son double,* with the important distinction that the cultivated person, unlike the martyr, can retain his physical integrity despite the flames around him.

Artaud's research into occult experience is neither the hedonistic experimentation of a lotus-eater nor the objective research of a scholar. It is a quest on which his very life depends, an urgent appeal to the world to offer him a context for unified being. This foundation must be the fruit of his own experience, and he must disseminate it to the world: "Pas possible ne trouve quoi à me répondre" (VIII, 61).[3] Ultimately, he finds that true culture abolishes the division between the sexes and the sexual conception of the child in order to create a race of one sex which gives birth to itself in organic unity. Hence, his search for culture fulfills not only the heteroplastic goal of action on the world, but the autoplastic desire to transform the conditions of his own being.

In seeking metaphysical truth, Artaud yields increasingly to the destiny which so preoccupies his texts concerning the Theater of Cruelty. He believes that universal forces will carry him forward to a loss of ego-consciousness, a merging of the self with the cosmos. This attitude, while a definition of mysticism, is saved from ephemerality by an ongoing and intensifying emphasis on the ontological status of the body. Concern with the physical side of life leads Artaud to advocate and depict that violence which takes corporeal experience to its farthest limits — as in Theater of Cruelty, but also in the peyote ritual of the Tarahumara Indians and the anarchic celebrations of the Roman emperor Heliogabalus.

Artaud's interest in non-Western and ancient cultures became an increasingly urgent preoccupation between 1933 and 1937, when his efforts to establish the Theater of Cruelty revealed to him the problems of modern Western civilization in a personal way. His readings in Taoism and the I Ching, the Upanishads and the Vedas, the Tibetan and Egyptian Books of the Dead, the Cabbala, Sufism, Tantric and Hatha Yoga, Greek mythology, the pre-Socratic philosophers, and finally, pre-Cortesian Mexican civilization[4] are noted in a section of Volume VIII. In these notes, Artaud follows Fabre d'Olivet, René Guénon, and the Japanese scholar Nyoiti Sakurazawa in attempting to create a synthesis of religious belief which would be meaningful for the contemporary West. His assimilation of these texts is creative as well as syncretic. For example, he follows Fabre d'Olivet in reversing the associations of *yin* and *yang* and notes that *yin*,* which is female and material in the Chinese tradition, should be male, while *yang* should be female and spiritual, in accord with the feminine *anima* of Greek tradition. Artaud searches for texts which appeal to his imagination, since he finds psychology and the delineation of character to be antihuman (VIII, 144). An example of his syncretism is the series of triads in which he equates the forces represented by the Christian trinity with Hindu, Aztec and Greek gods. The integration of religion and daily life into a unified culture is envisioned in the equation of divination with science in the I Ching and in the Vedic movement from text and ritual to revelation.

Ultimately, no single existing or recorded religious practice fulfills Artaud's desire for unity. The manic moments of Heliogabalus's reign

relationship with his protagonist point to identification: "Vrai ou non le personnage d'Héliogabale vit, je crois, jusque dans ses profondeurs, que ce soient celles d'Héliogabale personnage historique ou celles d'un personnage qui est moi" (VII, 185); "mais je finis tout de même par m'y rejoindre dans les détails de maints et maints passages, et dans la conception de la figure central où je me suis moi-même décrit" (VII, 187).[14] The depths of self and other which are proposed in the first passage and the word *rejoindre* in the second suggest the operation of a dialectic of historiographer and historical matter. At the time of composition, if not in his later life, Artaud was attracted to the figure of Heliogabalus as to a hollow shell which he can fill with his self.

A perpetual schism in the text between Artaud as creative historian and Artaud as narrator of himself leads to a fusion of subject and object and creates a unity in the text which reflects the evanescent and exalted unity in the life of Heliogabalus. *Héliogabale* may, therefore, be compared with *Les Cenci*, in which Artaud is likewise the author (and in this case, actor) of a character, Count Cenci, who is manifestly not the writer himself and yet who serves as a vehicle for Artaud's own ideas of cruelty and destiny. Hence, the life of Heliogabalus is a striking example of Theater of Cruelty transposed to life, for it retains a quality of manipulation and vicious humor which further allies it with theater.

At first glance, *Héliogabale* is a text of dualities opposed in binary sequence which consequently illustrates Artaud's highly dualistic worldview at this point in the evolution of his thought. The title is divided into two parts by the word *ou* (*or*), and each of these parts is further divided into opposing segments. "Heliogabalus," according to Artaud's extensive etymology, signifies a fusion of the high and the low, the earthly and the divine.[15] The alternative title, "the crowned anarchist," is an apparent oxymoron, but Artaud explains in the text that the crown and anarchy are fused in the reign of terror which occurs during Heliogabalus's tyranny. Although the work is composed of three chapters—"Le Berceau de sperme," "La Guerre des principes," and "L'Anarchie" ("The Cradle of Sperm," "The War of Principles," and "Anarchy")—the central chapter functions as the meeting place of two apparently dissimilar entities; it joins and separates them as does the "or" of the title. This pivotal chapter discusses a climax in the evolution of Western thought by exploring the alternatives which appeared at the time.

The two premises of the central chapter are that principles have real existence and that these principles war against one another. Moreover, the very existence of these principles reveals yet another duality: "Les principes ne valent que pour l'esprit qui pense, et quand il pense, mais hors de l'esprit qui pense, un principe se réduit à rien" (VII, 67).[16] Beyond this epistemological duality, there is a synthesis: "la Volonté dans l'Energie" ("Will in Energy," VII, 67); the human spirit remains the dominant element even in this union. In the sustained frenzy of Heliogabalus's reign, this point may have been attained. To the conflict of spirit and matter within man corresponds the duality of the human and the divine. Again, attention to pagan practice reveals a fusion of warring principles: "A l'origine de leurs croyances, il y a un terrible effort pour ne pas penser en hommes, pour garder le contact avec la création entière, c'est-à-dire avec la divinité" (VII, 60–61).[17] In its furthest extreme, this religious unity is expressed in the king, who traces his parentage to the gods and who proclaims his complete participation in both divine and human states. Just as the summit of humanity is the fusion of matter and spirit, so the highest perception of divinity is the great Whole which is Nothing (VII, 62). While the divine dialectic exists on a more abstract and grandiose plane than the human one, it still risks sliding into a perceptual void without the complementary synthesis in man. Human identity and divine otherness are aspects of a single indissoluble unity; neither can exist in the text of history without the other.

Nevertheless, it is neither on the plane of humanity nor on that of absolute divinity that the perpetual war of principles takes place. The combat zone is double: within the celebration of the divine, Artaud reveals a war of effigies; within the human world, this battle is doubled by a war between races which stand for the two cosmic principles, the male and the female. The situation represented by this war is erotic when the principles exist as separate, interacting entities, and it becomes androgynous when they fuse. But war only becomes violent when it is religious, when supernatural forces are explicitly engaged in human combat. The case of Heliogabalus, the pederast king who wanted to be a woman but who was also a priest of masculine deities, represents the archetypal war carried on within the human being itself. Every detail of Artaud's account reinforces this image of the individual *psychomachia* as a microcosmic example of the conflicts that occur on a universal scale.

Although in a strange and terrifying way Heliogabalus is a unity and represents the phantasmagorical specter of unity to his subjects, his actions are characterized by incessant duality. His behavior displays the unsettling quality of paradox: "Partout l'ampleur, l'excès, l'abondance, la démesure. La générosité et la pitié la plus pure qui viennent contrebalancer une spasmodique cruauté" (VII, 129).[18] In presenting such behavior, Artaud gives columnar examples of the double-edged nature of each of Heliogabalus's actions:

> Ordre, Désordre
> Unité, Anarchie
> Poésie, Dissonance
> Rythme, Discordance
> Grandeur, Puérilité
> Générosité, Cruauté. (VII, 127–28)[19]

However, the unity of Heliogabalus's world is such that these pairs are not contradictory: order and disorder participate in the same inferior level of action, unity is perceived through the generous and cruel operation of anarchy, and so forth. As in the case of Artaud's theatrical theory, new criteria for judgment are posited, and what is apparently contradictory becomes a vital fusion in the new unity.

At his point of explosive oneness, Heliogabalus turns the great temple of the sun at his home, Emesa, into a social reality. This temple, described at length early in the text in the course of his accession to power, serves as a vital metaphor for the life of the emperor. It is a sun temple built around a sacred "living stone" of phallic shape, but in juxtaposition with this image of height and masculinity are great sewers which surround it, and their mouths serve as gateways for the ritual servants (VII, 44–45). Within the sacred space of the temple, human excrement, blood, living humanity, concrete divinity, and the aura of the divine coexist and interact in an ascending operation that Artaud defines as "une idée de la transformation alchimique des sentiments en formes et des formes en sentiments . . . une idée de purification" (VII, 46).[20] Like Heliogabalus, the sun temple at Emesa fuses the masculine and the feminine at their extremes and represents at once the blackness and death that are the pitfalls of a sun-cult and the all-consuming "filtre pour le sang humain" of the gutters, with mouths which replicate the "O spasmodique du ciel" (VII, 48).[21]

Even at this early stage, Heliogabalus is capable of surmounting obstacles to unity, for, in an obvious analogy with the alchemical metaphor, one day "le sang du soleil monte en rosée dans sa tête, et chaque goutte de rosée solaire devient une énergie et une idée" (VII, 49). [22] By identifying himself with Elagabalus, the god of the temple, Heliogabalus overcomes the multiple divinities beneath and within the sun temple in order to achieve a "monothéisme magique, qui n'est pas seulement du verbe, mais de l'action" (VII, 50). [23] Monotheism, the mythical denial of plurality, is the unitary anarchy of the reign of Heliogabalus, and its result is a theater of blood, cruelty, and war.

Yet, at the height of his anarchic rule, Heliogabalus shows human weakness and falters. Having reached the paroxysm of ritual—poetry and theater—in the midst of an overwhelming consumption of goods and people, he cannot sustain the effort. Only when he is materially doubled by the child pretender Alexander Severus does he act, not as a unity, but as half of a duality. He attempts to have the child assassinated by the praetorian guards, but they turn against him. Joined by his terrified mother, Julia Soemia, Heliogabalus is linked *in extremis* with the woman who was responsible for his destiny and who will share his end. Heliogabalus flees and plunges into the guards' latrines. The symbolic quality of his death is an explicit function of the description of the Emesan sun-temple: alchemical purity is corrupted, the androgyne reverts to a "masculine" identity as the aggressor, then to a "feminine" action as the pursued, and finally to a grotesque figuration of sexual union. Heliogabalus is murdered by the guards at the latrines, but the desire of the crowds to shove him into the mouth of the sewer is thwarted because he is too broad-shouldered. The crowd attempts in vain to file down his shoulders and force him to enter; finally, they must throw him into the Tiber, where he floats with his mother out to sea.

Artaud found this conclusion so self-explanatory that it dispelled the need for further comment. On the other hand, Michel Foucault suggests that the text as a whole represents a rare and perhaps unique concretization of a fundamental principle of history:

La nécessité de la folie tout au long de l'histoire de l'Occident est liée à ce geste de décision qui détache du bruit de fond et de sa monotonie continue un langage significatif qui se transmet et s'achève dans le temps; bref, elle est liée à la possibilité de l'histoire. [24]

In the case of Heliogabalus, the context is displaced to the third century A.D., but Artaud emphasizes the tremendous pressure exerted by the Christian and Latin world on the pagan society represented by Heliogabalus. Thus the period of Heliogabalus's reign is an immensely fertile ground for historiography—the doubling of a nonrational subject with a nonrational text, as in the present case, may well be the only true history of Heliogabalus that could be written.

III *Satan*

In 1952, the writer Serge Berna was led by a ragpicker to an attic where, among scattered scraps of paper, he discovered the remains of several Artaud manuscripts.[25] The fragments are entitled "Vie et mort de Satan le Feu" ("Life and Death of the Late / Fire Satan"). The pun in the title, "le Feu," which means both "late" in the sense of deceased and "fire," is primary to the text itself, for the image of fire as rebellion which consumes itself and combines burning and death is the image of Satan himself. He is like a burning desert of Being which impedes human life through the "réfraction de la pensée satanique" (VIII, 123).[26] Satan is one identity of the sinister force which impedes the coincidence of thought and expression in the *Correspondance avec Jacques Rivière*. This conception of Satan is philosophically idealistic: "Car je tire de rien quelque chose et non de quelque chose *le Rien*" (VIII, 122).[27] Satan *is* in the world, not as an individual but as a living force.

The second text under the heading "Satan" is "Respiration," which is similar in subject to "Un Athlétisme affectif" (*Le Théâtre et son double*), but differs considerably in tone from the earlier essay. Unlike most of Artaud's writings, "Respiration" has an unusual poetic beauty; perhaps he found it too "pretty," too unlike his reality, for publication. The subject of Satan is present in the opposition of fire and ice (reminiscent of texts written ten years earlier) and in the depiction of the human soul as being divided between God and Satan. Artaud's cosmological vision is as dualistic here as in *Héliogabale*, but the most interesting division in terms of his later work concerns the self and the non-self. This duality is bridged by respiration; the movement of the respiratory system changes the configurations of self and world, at once uniting them and revealing their structures: "Et d'un seul mouvement voici que le système, gelé, montre ses arcanes semblables aux arcades d'un port qui relierait deux immensités" (VIII, 125).[28] "Affectively," as the earlier text states, breathing is the nexus of human life, a way to expel the influence of Satanic being.

But Satan, like the other representatives of religious systems which Artaud explored, recedes in the mid-1930s before his increasing interest in Mexico. During the period of his Mexican experience, Artaud discards syncretism for a single sacred system: that of the Tarahumara Indians as it is filtered through his own perceptions. When he rejects this religious philosophy in turn, he will move on to an original, personal framework of belief, rather than returning to his exploration of the occult.

CHAPTER 5

Mexico: The Magic Reality

ARTAUD defines the culture which he intends to find in Mexico in a text entitled "Le Mexique et la civilisation" ("Mexico and Civilization"), which was written before he left France and presented upon his arrival in Mexico.[1] The cultural principles are universal symbols with which the populace is confronted by the agency of a myth. In Mexican cultures, fires, especially in the form of the sun, is the dominant element—surely very attractive to Artaud, whose fascination with fire imagery from his early poems through *Le Théâtre et son double* is reinforced by its opposition of consuming change to the fatal stasis of ice. But the three remaining elements, earth, water, and air, are also represented in the Mexican pantheon; an example of their dynamic interaction is the Aztec god Quetzalcoatl, who as a winged serpent fuses air (wings) and earth (serpent). A second requisite configuration of cultural principles is astrological: "Toute vraie civilisation a ses bases dans l'astrologie et elle sait limiter au minimum ses catastrophes et ses crimes" (VIII, 413).[2] Again, Artaud's constant desire to prognosticate and to avoid accidental death finds a responsive voice in Mexican practice.

Perhaps the greatest asset of indigenous Mexican civilization for Artaud was that, unlike the subjects of his occult investigations, it really exists:

C'est peut-être une idée baroque pour un Européen, que d'aller rechercher au Mexique les bases vivantes d'une culture dont la notion semble s'effriter ici; mais j'avoue qui cette idée m'obsède; il y a au Mexique, liée au sol, perdue dans les coulées de lave volcanique, vibrante dans le sang indien, la réalité magique d'une culture, dont il faudrait peu de chose sans doute pour rallumer matériellement les feux. (VIII, 159)[3]

Despite the Spanish conquest and the ensuing years of Roman Catholic repression, Mexican cultures remain alive in their potential.

65

Unlike Christianity, which persisted and eventually exhausted such powers as it had, the Mayan, Aztec, and "Toltec" faiths were cut off in their prime and did not have time to die. Because Mexican gods are natural forces with incontrovertible appeal to both body and spirit, they maintain their power.

On a more metaphysical level, the Mexican cultures unite body and spirit as they fuse religion with the everyday; therefore, unlike European civilization, they are capable of generating a true human unity: "Une civilisation pour qui il y a le corps d'un côté et l'esprit de l'autre risque de voir à bref délai se détacher les liens qui unissent ces deux réalités dissemblables" (VIII, 161–62).[4] Even at this late date Artaud conceives of body and spirit in terms of Cartesian dualism, but he hopes, nonetheless, for their unification.

In several of the "revolutionary messages" which Artaud presented in lectures and articles in order to earn his livelihood and justify his mission to the official public, his reasons for coming to Mexico are explained in terms of his past work in theater. For example, the "Lettre ouverte aux Gouverneurs des Etats du Mexique" explains that the sacred rites and dances still practiced by remote Indian tribes are the greatest theatrical manifestations in the world. He contrasts governmental support given to young Mexican artists with the penury of their French counterparts (including himself) and calls upon the government to encourage, rather than repress, indigenous as well as "modern" culture. The European seeks contact with natural forces through Mexican culture and is confused and disappointed when he finds that Mexicans are more interested in his culture than in their own. According to Artaud, European art is in a state of "social anarchy," and the artists themselves are largely responsible; hence, it would be a grave error for the Mexican artist to imitate the degenerate European.

But Artaud did not go to Mexico as an artist: "Je suis venu au Mexique chercher une nouvelle idée de l'homme" (VIII, 260).[5] As a result, the texts which relate to his experiences among the Indians of the remote Sierra Tarahumara may not be described as poetry or prose fiction, but rather they stand as testimony and analysis of the "new man" revealed to him in the culture of these apparently primitive people.

I   The Tarahumaras

The texts collected by Artaud's editor under the title *Les Tarahumaras* were written over a period of eight years and in four distinct surroundings: while "La Montagne des signes" ("The Mountain of Signs") was written in Mexico itself around October 1936 and "D'un voyage au pays des Tarahumaras" ("Of a Voyage to the Land of the Tarahumaras") apparently in Paris shortly after his return, "Le Rite du peyotl chez les Tarahumaras" ("The Peyote Rite Among the Tarahumaras") was written while Artaud was in the asylum at Rodez in 1943, and "Tutuguri," one of his last texts, dates from February 12, 1948, when he lived in freedom at Ivry. The publishing history of these texts is quite complex and reflects upon the writings themselves, especially in view of Artaud's virulent rejection of Christianity, expressed in a letter to Henri Parisot and in the "Postscript" which are included among the texts.[6]

The order in which the texts appear was established by Artaud (see IX, 242); it is not chronological in terms of the events described or in the composition of the texts. Their relationship is arbitrary despite the unifying element of Artaud's experiences among the Tarahumara Indians, for these experiences are often used as premises for wide-ranging speculation. Yet, more than any of the diverse cultures explored by Artaud, the Tarahumaran is a personal revelation of a culture which not only fulfills all of his prerequisites, but which also suggests possibilities beyond even his fertile imagination. In a letter to Jean Paulhan after his return, he writes that he is "*conduit par l'Invisible comme je sens que toute ma vie est conduite actuellement*" (IX, 132).[7] He need search no longer among the dusty archives of the world's dead religions, for Truth has been revealed to him with the terrifying brilliance of Tutuguri, the black sun.

Les Tarahumaras is as generically unclassifiable as *Héliogabale*, and it even resembles the latter text somewhat in its mixture of essay, narrative, and exalted personal witness. In general terms, *Les Tarahumaras* bears the same relation to ethnography as *Héliogabale* to historiography, especially in terms of Jacques Derrida's definition: "Cette archéologie est aussi une téléologie et une eschatologie; rêve d'une présence pleine et immédiate fermant l'histoire; transparence et indivision d'une parousie, suppression de la contradiction et de la différence."[8] The "mountain of signs," the peyote rite, and the very clothing of the Tarahumaras represent a synthesis and a transcendence of the many faiths Artaud explored, at once confirming them and pointing to a still higher metaphysical reality. The subsequent revisions and retractions which efface specific references, especially those to Christianity, only heighten the impact of the greater revelation. The rejected gods will return in force to torment Artaud during

the latter half of the twelve-year period during which *Les
Tarahumaras* was composed. Between "La Montagne des signes"
and "Tutuguri," confident optimism was overwhelmed by a black
vision of the void within himself.

The conclusion and "Post-scriptum" to *Les Tarahumaras* comment
upon the circumstances in which it was written. Like the *Lettres de
Rodez* (*Letters from Rodez*), they detail a litany of the tortures which
Artaud has undergone. Finally, there is an anti-Christian complaint:
Artaud says that because he was converted to Christianity by the
sorcery of priests, he used the ignobly sexual sign of the cross,
especially in the lost (or destroyed) original version of "Le Rite du
peyotl." The rather embarrassed denial of Christianity echoes his
more virulent letter to Henri Parisot (September 1945), which
appears in *Les Tarahumaras* as a repudiation of the "Supplément au
Voyage au pays des Tarahumaras" written in January 1944. At this
time (1945), Artaud also wrote "god" and "christ" without capital
letters; later texts degrade the spelling of Christian references even
further.

"Supplément au Voyage au pays des Tarahumaras" interprets the
Mexican experience in light of a quasi-Christian mysticism; his
interrogation of the world is directed by God through a cruciform
opening of perception. From this point of view, Christ is the source of
the Ciguri initiation, for he appeared to the ancient Tarahumaras
(their descendants identified an "authentic picture" of Jesus) and
gave them Ciguri. At the core of peyote, Christ reveals a combat of
wills within Artaud in which he fights off external forces that try to
pollute his consciousness with eroticism and advances toward the
existence which is absolutely Good. The "God of Eternal Charity"
which he was predestined to find through the peyote ritual is also the
object of his trip to Ireland in the following year.

When Artaud repudiated the "Supplement" in his 1945 letter to
Parisot, it was the Christian implications which aroused his strongest
antagonism: "Le christ est ce que j'ai toujours le plus abominé" (IX,
63).[9] He abjures Christianity in favor of a Christlike self-evaluation.
Not only is his own suffering an index of his election, but he is also
convinced that his birth was, like that of Jesus, asexual:

C'est vous dire que ce n'est pas Jésus-christ que je suis allé chercher chez les
Tarahumaras mais moi-même, moi, Mr. Antonin Artaud né le 4 septembre
1896 d'un utérus où je n'avais que faire et dont je n'ai jamais rien eu à faire
même avant, parce que ce n'est pas une façon de naître, que d'être copulét

masturbé 9 mois par la membrane, la membrane brillante qui dévore sans dents comme disent les UPANISHADS, et je sais que j'étais né autrement. (IX, 64–65)[10]

Rejection of Christianity is therefore rejection of the mother as well as of the father, and the rejection of sexual generation implied by the parents remains a constant motif in the most literal sense in Artaud's later texts.

"Le Rite du peyotl chez les Tarahumaras" (1943) begins with the phrase "comme j'ai déjà dit" (IX, 13), a phrase which is at once an index of the volume's nonlinearity and an assertion of authority, for Artaud had previously written about the Tarahumaras and assumes that the reader is familiar with these prior publications. The account is a "reconstruction" rather than reportage, and its distance from the factual experience which serves as its subject is a function not only of the passage of time, but also of the experience of the peyote itself and of the six years spent in institutions for the insane. The intensity of Artaud's experience with peyote may well have increased with his temporal distance from it; although he still gives many ethnological details, they are outweighed by the glory and terror of his confrontation with Ciguri, the god within the mushroom.

The Tarahumaran worldview is dominated by two concepts of god: the Master of All Things, who rules the multiplicity of external human relationships, and Tutuguri, the (black) sun, who is an overwhelming unity. The narrative line of this text concerns Artaud's passage from multiplicity to Tutuguri's unity through the agency of Ciguri, that is, peyote, in a nightlong ritual. A fourth divine image which reappears in Artaud's texts outside the Mexican experience is revealed in the peyote dance: "La figure des opérations extrêmes par lesquelles L'HOMME PERE, NI HOMME NI FEMME a tout créé" (IX, 15).[11] Like the cruelty of Artaud's theater, this divine figure is perceived by its action on the body and nervous system. This latter deity is the effective force of the unity represented by Tutuguri. Hence, the metaphysics of Artaud's Tarahumaras may be seen as follows:

SEE NEXT PAGE FOR DIAGRAM

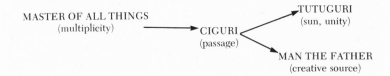

By yielding to Ciguri and abandoning consciousness, the Indian sees the image of God's infinite power within himself. Like Artaud, he finds in the Ciguri ritual "une rite de création et qui explique comment les choses *sont* dans le Vide et celui-ci dans l'Infini, et comment elles en sortirent dans la Réalité, et furent faites" (IX, 25).[12] Cirguri is, however, a mutilated image, for the man who constructed himself out of his own body was assassinated by a cruel and jealous God. While Ciguri retains its power of transformation, in the privileged circumstances of the dance it also reveals its mutilation: "Car je crus voir dans cette Danse le point où l'inconscient universel est malade" (IX, 28).[13]

The figure which dominates the peyote dance is the number 8, which traced in the air and on the earth, corresponds exactly in symbology to the intermediate status of Ciguri: 8 is "the intermediate form between the square (or the terrestrial order) and the circle (the eternal order) and is, in consequence, a symbol of regeneration."[14] It is also the double sigmoid, the common symbol for infinity. Thus Ciguri, the figure 8, is a fusion of natural and spiritual forces in opposition to 0, which stands for Tutuguri and is both unity (the circle) and the void (zero), as well as a symbolic representation of eternity. On the other hand, in "La Danse du peyotl," the importance of the ritual space as a magic circle is emphasized. The 8 also resembles the magic figure of two triangles connected at their points (X) which stands, according to Artaud, for the tree of life as it passes through the center of reality.

Peyote reveals the self as well as the cosmos to those who use it properly. Ciguri, the self-created, mutilated man, is Artaud himself, for, when he sees Ciguri, it is in the letters "JE" ("I"):

Du côté où était ma rate un vide immense se creusa qui se peignit en gris et rose comme la rive de la mer. Et au fond de ce vide apparut la forme d'une racine échourée, une sorte de J qui aurait eu à son sommet trois branches surmontées d'un E triste et brillant comme un oeil. Des flammes sortirent de l'oreille gauche du J et passant par derrière lui semblèrent pousser toutes les choses à droite, du côté où était mon foie, mais très au delà de lui. Je n'en vis pas plus et tout s'évanouit ou ce fut moi qui m'évanouis en revenant à la réalité ordinaire. En tout cas j'avais vu, paraît-il, l'Esprit même de Ciguri. (IX, 133)[15]

Although this powerful experience does not protect him from belief in false sensations and perceptions (cf. IX, 35), such as the feeling that the demons who surround him can be chased away with the sign of the cross, it does keep his reason intact so long as he is safe from starvation and poisoning.

The earlier "Danse du peyotl" is more identifiable as description and interpretation of an experience. Before attaining the revelation of the peyote ritual, Artaud must endure twenty-eight days of suffering brought on by the hostility of the mountain itself toward him; it wants to keep the creative power of peyote from him, but he persists and wins out. Having presented the metaphysical meaning of the ritual in the 1943 text, Artaud places the earlier essay afterwards because its wealth of factual detail establishes a priority in favor of the spiritual meaning of ritual over its ethnological implications.

The peyote dancers arrive in a vision which Artaud compares with Hieronymous Bosch's *Nativity*: the men carry upright crosses, while the women are burdened with ceremonial paraphernalia. As the dance begins, a circle is traced in the earth and the women grind the peyote. This magic circle defines sacred space; outside, space is "morally deserted" and dancers who set foot there are prey to the basest of human functions. One cruciform tree is hung with the lungs and hearts of goats, another with mirrors which reflect the firelight. Both light and sound play among the crosses, which are hung with bells placed at the east; they represent the ten masters of peyote. Fusion of the sexes, found in the figure of "Man the Father," appears in the hermaphroditic peyote root which lies in a hole at the feet of each dancer. On top of the covered root, the sorcerer-priest grates more peyote, thereby dislocating the principles in the realm of the abstract while they lie together in the concrete.[16]

There are twelve phases in the dancing during which the celebrants pass around the circle between the two "suns," which are represented by the glittering crosses and which are associated with the passage from sunset to sunrise. At dawn, the dancers spit out the remaining peyote, while Artaud is led to the crosses for the "final cure"

(IX, 158). The sacred rasp is placed on his head, he is washed and sprinkled, and he sees behind the ritual the Principal who guarantees that his suffering has not been in vain.

From this point to the end of the essay, the text is more concerned with Artaud than with the peyote ritual. For him, the experience was like a flaming crucifixion which released the powers of Ciguri: "J'étais prêt à toutes les brûlures, et j'attendais les premices de la brûlure, en vue d'une combustion bientôt généralisée" (IX, 62).[17] In the exemplary theatrical experience of the peyote ritual, he has become the martyr who signals through the flames and whose communication is valued above words in the preface to Le Théâtre et son double.

Three phases in Artaud's self-concept are represented in the three texts on the peyote dance. While in the 1936 text, he experiences a mystical union with the "Principal" which leads him to conclude that his experience has eschatological implications for the entire world, in the second, his physical being is identified with Christ-Ciguri, and in the third—he is God. The latter text, like "Tutuguri," includes the glossolalic syllables of Artaud's invented language. In French, he states that under the influence of peyote he understood that he had invented life and was given the imagination to do so. As the holder of the command-switch to the real machinery of the world, Artaud exercises an enigmatic quality which he calls "l'humour-né" ("born-humor"). This force is the ironic action of the cruel creator whose jokes on humanity are not generally recognized; "born-humor" is the humor of the initiated. Like the glossolalic syllables, it is a common feature of Artaud's later texts, and its presence in "Une Note sur le peyotl" creates a continuity between the Tarahumaran period and the time which stretches from Artaud's release from Rodez to his death.

The "stage" for Artaud's experiences among the Tarahumaras is prepared by a series of essays which describe and interpret the Sierra Tarahumara landscape and the Indians' racial identity. Written while Artaud was in Mexico and immediately after his return to Paris, these texts ("La Montagne des signes," "Le Pays des Rois-Mages," "Une Race-principe," "Le Rite des Rois de l'Atlantide," and "La Race des hommes perdus") are less exalted and less personal in tone than the later texts and derive largely from Artaud's search for a synthetic culture.

"La Montagne des signes" ("The Mountain of Signs") was written on Sierra Tarahumara itself and published along with "La Danse du peyotl" in the Nouvelle Revue Française on August 1, 1937. By far the most interesting of the texts not directly connected with Tarahumaran ritual, it describes and interprets the overwhelming unity of Indian culture with its setting in a manner reminiscent of the opening section of *Héliogabale*. The gods may be jealous of their power, but their mere presence is enough to give the traveler hope:

Le pays des Tarahumaras est plein de signes, de formes, d'effigies naturelles qui ne semblent point nés du hasard, comme si les dieux, qu'on sent partout ici, avaient voulu signifier leurs pouvoirs dans ces étranges signatures où c'est la figure de l'homme qui est de toutes parts pourchassée. (IX, 43)[18]

The figure of man is in direct conflict with the gods, and, like the Ciguri vision of the opening text, it reveals a sacrificial superman who is, again, Artaud himself. The rock formation of a man standing next to a window in which the sun and moon describe their course leads to the figure of "Man the Father" which will appear in Artaud's peyote vision as the mutilated but potentially omnipotent ruler of the cosmos. Other formations are analyzed as being forms which return to their real essences: a female chest, voracious animal heads, and phallic rocks reveal "une histoire d'enfantement dans la guerre, une histoire de genèse et de chaos" (IX, 46).[19] The landscape shows Artaud his own life in a cosmological context.

As he penetrates the mystery of the rock formations, Artaud finds that they are not all natural: "Cette Sierra habitée et qui souffle une pensée métaphysique dans ses rochers, les Tarahumaras l'ont semée de signes, de signes parfaitement conscients, intelligents et concertés" (IX, 47).[20] The most striking of these man-made signs is a detached letter H (H), enclosed in a circle, which Artaud will describe elsewhere as the representation of male and female sexuality in confrontation.[21] In "La Montagne des signes" and "Au pays des Rois-Mages," the whole gamut of universal hieroglyphic symbolism is associated with the Tarahumaras: along with figure 8 or double triangle and the circle described in relation to the peyote dance, Artaud finds crosses, swords, trefoils, the ankh, the swastika, the double cross, large circles with points at their centers, figures of three points, four triangles at the four cardinal points, and the twelve signs of the zodiac. In a letter to Paulhan, he explains that he was told that these signs were "les Signes d'un langage basé sur la forme même du souffle quand il se dégage en sonorités" (IX, 124)[22]—that is, a solution to the problem of the annotation of nonlinguistic phenomena for the stage.

This symbolic conjunction points to a unity of "true culture" which

finds expression in varying forms in all civilizations. Hence, the
conclusion of "La Montagne des signes" finds Tarahumaran culture
valuable and surprisingly similar to more familiar cultures:

Et il me paraît étrange que le peuple primitif des Tarahumaras, dont les rites
et dont la pensée sont plus vieux que le Déluge, ait pu déjà posséder cette
science bien avant que la Légende du Graal apparût, bien avant que se formât
la Secte des Rose-Croix. (IX, 48)[23]

This interpretation of Tarahumaran culture is expanded in three
texts which appeared in the Mexican newspaper *El Nacional* while
Artaud was in Mexico. The original French versions have been lost,
and it is likely that they read quite differently before the double
translation which returned them to French, but we may assume that
the ideas, which show considerable continuity with other contemporary texts, remain intact. "Le Pays des Rois-Mages" ("The Land of
the Magi"), like "La Montagne des signes" in that it was written on
Sierra Tarahumara, bears a striking resemblance to the "Supplément" in its use of Christian myth. According to this text, Tarahumaran iconography and legend depict the Nativity and the Magi who
spread the sun cult because the two legends share a preoccupation
with the search for essentials:

Dans la montagne tarahumara tout ne parle que de l'Essentiel, c'est-à-dire
des principes suivant lesquels la Nature s'est formée; et tout ne vit que pour
ces principes: les Hommes, les orages, le vent, le silence, le soleil. (IX, 45)[24]

Hence, the humanism of the Renaissance, which brought nature
under human control, was a step backward. The humanists' exclusive consideration of man has led to a loss of the natural. The idea that
humanity must rise to the level of nature rather than reduce it to
human scale is also emphasized in a statement set on a single page
after "Le Pays des Rois-Mages": "La Nature a produit les danseurs
dans leur cercle comme elle produit le maïs dans son cercle et les
signes dans les forêts" (IX, 82).[25] By following the forces of nature,
humanity will find true culture.

"Une Race-Principe" ("A Principle-Race"), also written in Mexico,
is another text of metaphysical interpretation according to the evi-
dence furnished by Artaud's experiences among the Tarahumaras
and their links with other cultures. The apparently coincidental use of
a double-pointed headdress, for example, is found to be a link to the

original Male-Female force and resembles those worn by the pharaohs, Moses, the ancient Chinese, and the Mayas. The cross suggests not only Christian associations but also that "ici l'espace géométrique est vivant, il a produit ce qu'il y a de mieux, c'est-à-dire l'homme" (IX, 86).[26] Many aspects of Artaud's own metaphysics appear in this text attributed to the Tarahumaras: belief in the Double, superiority of consciousness over morality, obsession with the philosophical meaning of gesture, and a recurrent motif of war between Male and Female principles which are presently in a state of unnatural balance.

One more link between the Tarahumaras and world mythology is made in "Le Rite des Rois de l'Atlantide" ("The Rite of the Kings of Atlantis"), in which a Tarahumaran ritual is found to duplicate that of the Atlantean kings as described in Plato's *Critias*. Artaud's immediate and rather sensationalist conclusion is that the Tarahumaras are the long-sought descendants of the lost continent. Hence, theirs is a "true tradition" and one more valid than Western progress because they represent for all eternity the most advanced truth that exists. The ritual in question involves drinking the blood of bulls to the accompaniment of melancholy songs at sunset and the invocation of the sun; the dance itself is described extensively. In the conclusion of the article, Artaud qualifies his assertion of the Tarahumaras' descent: "L'idée de ce rite sacré leur vint de la même source fabuleuse et préhistorique" as that of the Atlanteans (IX, 93).[27]

A more general and superficial account of the Tarahumaras appears in "La Race des hommes perdus" ("The Race of the Lost Men"), which was first published in 1937 in the magazine *Voilà* under the pseudonym John Forester. A certain amount of realism appears in Artaud's allusion to the Tarahumaras' poverty, which he explains as a function of their disdain for the everyday realities of civilization.[28] There follows a brief description of the peyote initiation rite in which the magic rasp is emphasized.

In contrast with these alternately repetitive and fantastic journalistic essays, "Tutuguri" has the strength and urgency of Artaud's late texts; indeed, it was written on February 16, 1948, less than a month before his death.[29] While "La Danse du peyotl chez les Tarahumaras" is under the sign of Ciguri, the peyote-god who represents immediate transformational experience, "Tutuguri" describes the ritual of the black sun, "le Rite de la nuit noire et de la mort *éternelle* du soleil" (IX, 69).[30] The free verse and anguished tone of this text further set it

apart from the rest of *Les Tarahumaras*. In an accompanying letter to
Marc Barbezat, Artaud explains that it was written after three attacks
of syncope and loss of blood.

At the beginning of the Tutuguri ritual, six men carrying crosses
appear, while a seventh holds a strange booming musical instrument
later identified as a tympanum. Then a strong wind arises and brings a
face which demands chastity. As dawn breaks, a flame erupts in a
circle and becomes the sun, which boils with a terrifying sound. The
six crosses burn and the six men fall to the ground in exhaustion. In
juxtaposition with the sixfold rhythm of these men, the drum-player
represents Tutuguri, for the hollow drum is the sound of the void. A
vision appears, as intense and powerful as that of "La Danse du
peyotl," in which Tutuguri takes human form and becomes Artaud
himself:

> ... le cheval avançant porte sur lui le tronc d'un homme
> d'un homme nu et qui brandit
> non pas une croix
> mais un bâton de bois de fer
> attaché à un gigantesque fer à cheval
> où son corps tout entier passe
> son corps taillé d'une balafre de sang
> et le fer à cheval est là
> comme les mâchoires d'un carcan,
> que l'homme eût pris
> à la balafre de son sang. (IX, 73–74)[31]

This remarkable figure suggests yet another recurrence of Artaud's
preoccupation with generation and birth, for the horseshoe represents the power of the mother which remains in force despite her
secondary place with regard to the man himself.

Despite its thematic unity, *Les Tarahumaras* is an extremely
diverse collection which refutes "topical" coherence in Artaud's
texts. From extremely personal statement in "La Danse du peyotl"
and "Tutuguri" through the mass-market journalism of the texts in *El
Nacional* and the pseudonymous "Race des hommes perdus" to the
anonymously published "Montagne des signes" and "Rite du peyotl,"
the very relationship of writer and text changes dramatically. In fact,
"Tutuguri" was dictated and not written down at all by Artaud. He
also moves from the syncretic mythology which finds points of
reference in Tarahumaran ritual to an entirely individual response
which is even broader in its metaphysical implications than the

universal symbology of the "mountain of signs." Between the earliest and latest texts in this volume, Artaud vehemently rejected the occultism which so enthralled him and adopted instead a worldview based entirely on his physical being. Before he abandoned occultism, however, Artaud wrote *Les Nouvelles Révélations de l'Etre (The New Revelations of Being)*, a text more exalted and confident than those in *Les Tarahumaras*.

II   *The Revelation*

Les Nouvelles Révélations de l'Etre was published on July 28, 1937, over the signature "Le Révélé" ("The Revealed One"). It is based primarily on astrology, in which Artaud had long been interested, and on the tarot, which he had studied in the late spring of the same year.[32] The central portion of the text is an astrological-tarot interpretation of the metaphysical climate on June 19, 1937. It is complemented by an introduction of the "revealed" persona, an explanation of the text's messianic voice in the guise of "Le Torturé" ("The Tortured One"), and a conclusion which predicts the destruction of the world. Despite the complex and sybilline language of this text, the message is clear: the world is coming to an end, and humanity is doomed unless it follows the revelations.

In the period between his return to Mexico and his departure for Ireland, Artaud insisted on anonymity. "Mon nom doit disparaître," he wrote to Jean Paulhan, not only in order to express himself freely, but also because "dans peu de temps je serai mort ou alors dans une situation telle que de toute façon je n'aurai pas besoin de nom" (VII, 223, 227).[33] His messianic fervor, his belief that he had found the true Way, at once transcended his erstwhile identity and was somewhat dangerous to express. In three opening epigrams, a structure of combat and confusion is established; first the elements are mixed, then the populace set against one another, and finally a mother eats her sons. The conclusion to this opening sequence is that without war there is no stability (VII, 146).

Les Nouvelles Révélations gives the dates of a rapid succession of events at the end of which, on November 7, 1937, "le Torturé est devenu pour tout le monde le Reconnu, LE REVELE" (VII, 174).[34] The world failed to come to an end, but Artaud's own world was brutally cut off before the prophesized events could come to pass, for on September 29, he was arrested on board ship and began his nine-year torment in insane asylums. The violence and confidence of *Les Nouvelles Révélations* are consequently tinged with poignance.

There is, however, no sentimentality in the persona of "The Revealed One" who writes in the text: "Je dis ce que j'ai vu et ce que je crois; et qui dira que je n'ai pas vu ce que j'ai vu, je lui déchire maintenant la tête" (VII, 149).[35] He has yielded to the Void and cut himself off from the world. Yet, he is not like the normally dead, who turn about in their cadavers, for his Being endures in the world as his Double.

The tarot-based interpretation of the astrological situation on June 19, 1937, is divided into the traditional ternaries and quarternaries under the headings of heaven, earth, and hell. The message is at once grim and unambiguous: the Male in its widest incarnation will overcome the influence of the Female, and the analogous Right will submerge the Left. Not only will female sexuality, for which much of the world's evil is blamed, be extinguished by male dominance, but also the political left—republics and democracies—will vanish in a wave which represses the masses. At another point, however, Artaud insists that "la Droite à laquelle je pense est la Droite de l'Homme et non la stupide Réaction" (VII, 242, letter to André Breton).[36] Although the sexual implications of this prediction are impossible to verify, the political forecast is entirely accurate (the disclaimer to Breton not withstanding), even a possible foregone conclusion in light of the contemporary rise of fascism. "Nous sommes menacés d'esclavage," the Revealed One interprets, "parce que la Nature va retomber sur nous" (VII, 160).[37] The Revolution (a "female" event) will be enacted by a male directing force; it will reinstate the kings who are now slaves, and life will desert humanity, leaving it in hell.

The male in question is "a mad-wise man," the Tortured One who holds the cane and sword which depict in numerological terms the dates of important upcoming events.[38] The "abstract being" which declared the sexes separate now holds the key to the world's destiny. His ineffable dream implies the eternal chastity of both sexes, as well as the sweeping movement of justice. The persona who is the subject of this interpretation is not merely the Tortured One; he is also "the Juggler" who will avenge the evil spread by women: "Un cycle du monde est achevé" (VII, 160);[39] the juggler's balls will return in a new world-shape.

In the conclusion, the motif of elemental destruction is repeated with the addition of a star which takes over the atmosphere. Despite the apparent confusion, the devastation preached by the Revealed One is conscious (VII, 173). All things will be burned, not by fire, but by Earth, and the process will have begun by the time *Les Nouvelles*

Révélations de l'Etre is published: "Le 25 juillet 1937, le Macrocosme a rencontré la Terre" (VII, 174).[40] When, on November 7, the cataclysm occurs, the Tortured One—the Juggler, the Revealed One—will accede to his foreordained position and lead the world through the ensuing chaos.[41]

But the Tortured One was to remain unrecognized, at least for the next nine years. After an ill-starred trip to Ireland, where he sought the source of the power of Saint Patrick's cane, Artaud was imprisoned, first by the police, then by the State. The war that he predicted would come, but his own war was with psychiatrists and demons.

CHAPTER 6

Pain and Authenticity

ANTONIN Artaud's search for an existing cultural matrix which would give him sufficient scope to exercise his beliefs was ultimately in vain. Even the exultation he experienced among the Tarahumaras and the inspiration he drew from the learning of non-Western religions failed to satisfy him, for in these cultures, the individual is lost in the workings of a foreordained worldview. But outside religious contexts, in the realm of art, Artaud finds another way to define his place in the world. He is not the only one who suffers or creates in an authentic manner.

The greatest number of texts by the mature Artaud on the subject of other writers appears in the period when he was shut up as a madman or are directly related to this period. Far from being paradoxical, the link between the diagnosis of madness and the evaluation of other artists is intrinsic to Artaud's writing. While the question of Artaud's madness may be of dubious value to the analysis and appreciation of his writing, the urgent questions which his mental health inspired him to pose are of interest: who am I? who is torturing me? why am I being tortured? what is my mind? what is my body? how do they exist? how can my terrible suffering be changed?

Artaud's approaches to these problems describe a distinct trajectory, from simple awareness of their existence through facile answers borrowed from Christian and heretical dogmas to highly individual responses which react violently to the suggestion that urgent questions can be resolved through any experience which is not strictly personal. Nevertheless, he finds analogies in the writing and painting of others who he thinks have suffered as he does. Finally, after his emergence from the institutions, Artaud presents a forceful argument for his point of view in *Van Gogh, le suicidé de la société* (*Van Gogh, Society's Suicide,* 1947).

The first part of Artaud's *via dolorosa* in asylums found him stifled

80

by the terrible conditions in French institutions during World War II, as well as by his own ill health. Although he corresponded from the asylum at Ville-Evrard, these letters were intercepted by asylum authorities and often were never delivered. A reconstruction of their contents depicts an Artaud who is prey to the religious fervor which obsessed him in the late 1930s, with the notable difference that the religion in question is Catholicism. Artaud's conversion during his Irish trip lasted well into 1943, and Christianity lost its hold on him only after his transfer to the asylum to Rodez.

Whether or not the move to Rodez changed Artaud for the better—and controversy continues on this topic[1]—it indisputably altered his relationship with the outside world. The letters which poured forth from Rodez repeatedly and emphatically reveal the workings of a mind which is so unlike the conventional model of psychic normality that it frightens and alienates the unprepared observer.

While Artaud's Rodez letters take him further from literary normality, they bring him closer to his chosen predecessors. The epistolary form, even in its most uncertain state, assures Artaud that he may communicate; like a dramatic performance, a letter is defined by the presence of a hypothetical audience. The letters and other texts which have as their subjects other artists are, therefore, not the involuted writings of a critic, but performance texts in the same sense as his later poems.

I   *Gérard de Nerval*

Of all his predecessors, Artaud expresses his deepest affinity with Gérard de Nerval. While allusions to Nerval appear in several earlier texts, his best-known commentary is found in a letter written at Rodez on Nerval's collection of poetry, *Les Chimères*. Entitled "Sur les Chimères"[2] the text was written (but never mailed) to the critic Georges Le Breton in response to an article which appeared in the review *Fontaine* in the summer of 1945.[3]

As part of a current of interest in Nerval as a poet with occult implications, Le Breton's essay interprets Nerval's work in light of various "sources"; he finds keys to *Les Chimères* in the imagery of alchemy. According to Artaud, this approach is not merely misleading, but pernicious. The poet creates mythology; he does not mimic alchemy, but surpasses its failures.[4] The creatures who go by familiar names in Nerval's poetry are not borrowings but his own creations:

"Les êtres nés dans la tuméfiante escharre de-son coeur d'immortel suicidé qui viennent bramer au premier plan leur drame, la tragédie de leur volonté de clarté" (XI, 197).[5]

Artaud violently denounces Le Breton and source criticism in general:

Cet esprit de'éternelle paresse qui toujours devant la douleur, et dans la crainte d'y entrer de trop près, je veux dire de *connaître* l'âme de Gérard de Nerval, comme on connaît les bubons d'une peste . . . s'est réfugié dans la critique des sources. (XI, 187–88)[6]

Artaud's argument places Nerval in a dominant position in relation to mythology and the occult. In the following statement, the words *repris (taken back), revendiqués (reclaimed),* and *sauvés (saved)* indicate a disparity which Artaud perceives as radically separating the territory of poetry from the domain of the common unconscious as expressed in hermetic symbolism: "Gérard de Nerval du sein de ses tumeurs d'esprit est parvenu à faire vivre des êtres, êtres par lui à l'alchimie repris, et qu'il a revendiqués aux Mythes, et sauvés de l'ensevelissement des Tarots" (XI, 184–85).[7] It is as if the whole cast of mythic beings in *Les Chimères* were rescued once and for all from drowning in the murky irreality of the occult.

For Artaud, Le Breton's use of alchemical imagery as a key to *Les Chimères* is a reversal, for Nerval's poetry comes closer to realizing the "Grand Oeuvre" of the alchemists than the efforts of the "so-called science" of alchemy (XI, 188). Poetry like Nerval's has the absolute newness of the product sought by alchemists but, unlike their goal, it actually exists.

What do these references mean in Nerval's poetry if they do not allude to their erstwhile mythical context? According to Artaud, for whom life and literature cannot be separated, there can be only one answer: these proper nouns are "d'insolites et merveilleuses machines de conscience" (XI, 190),[8] which *mean* Nerval himself. Artaud's discussion centers on the poem "Antéros," and it is evident that he has no interest in the myths attached to the character Antaeus, for all his allusions are to the poem and to the poet, not to their namesakes. Antaeus, Dagon, Baal do not participate in "des histoires louches de la Fable" ("shady stories of Fables"); rather, they translate the anguish of "Gérard de Nerval, pendu un matin et rien de plus" (XI, 185).[9]

Consequently, it is not enough that a great poet act upon myths and transform them into his own highly personal property. The greatest transfiguration derives from the fact that Nerval hanged himself. Artaud's insistence upon Nerval's suicide as a cornerstone of his reading of "Antéros" is based directly on the text, specifically the second line, "Et sur un col flexible une tête indomptée" ("And an uncontrollable head on a flexible neck"). This line suggests the physical position of the man who has hanged himself as an act of revolt against the world: while the neck may be twisted, the head remains unbowed.

The reader who wishes to understand *Les Chimères* must, according to Artaud, look into Nerval's soul with empathy. Only by rejecting source criticism can we enter into the more valuable reaches of Nerval's mind. However, Nerval's poetry attains this clarity only when read aloud; Artaud's theories of breath control and enunciation, which are of great importance in *Le Théâtre et son double,* are applied to Nerval's work as part of the argument:

La preuve du sens des vers des *Chimères* ne peut être fait par la Mythologie . . . mais uniquement par la diction . . . à condition d'être de nouveau et à chaque lecture, *expectorées.* —Car c'est alors que leurs hiéroglyphes deviennent clairs. (XI, 187)[10]

Artaud's practice of this technique is verified by an anecdote recounted by Paule Thévenin. Her concierge had intercepted Artaud in order to reproach him because his reading of Nerval on the preceding evening had disturbed Mme Thévenin's neighbors: "A peine eut-elle ouvert la bouche qu'il l'arrêta: 'Taisez-vous! si vous persistez à m'interdire de déclamer les vers de Gérard de Nerval, je vous change immédiatement en serpent á tête plate'."[11] That Artaud was making the same type of effort at Rodez is evidenced by a letter to Roger Blin, but he notes that a performance there was unsuccessful (XI, 217–18).

While Nerval is certainly Artaud's preferred predecessor, he is not the only creative artist whom Artaud enshrines in the pantheon of *poètes maudits.* Baudelaire, Poe, and Lautréamont fulfill his criteria, along with the painter Vincent Van Gogh.

II *Authentic and Inauthentic Writing*

For Artaud, pain is a touchstone for the evaluation of literature, and he therefore tests the works of various writers with this critical litmus in his letters from Rodez:

Tout ce qui n'est pas un tétanos de l'âme ou ne vient pas d'un tétanos de l'âme comme les poèmes de Baudelaire ou d'Edgar Poe n'est pas vrai et ne peut pas être reçu dans la poésie. (IX, 184–85)

J'aime les poèmes . . . des suppliciés du langage qui sont en perte de leurs écrits. (IX, 186)

Un poème qui ne vient pas de la douleur m'ennuie, un poème fait avec tous les superflus de l'être . . . m'exaspère. (IX, 227)[12]

Not to suffer is to give tacit consent to the scandal of language, which limits human freedom by virtue of its origin: "Il n'est pas une de nos paroles qui dans notre bouche vit autrement que *décollé des cieux*."[13]

Artaud denounces Lewis Carroll's "Jabberwocky" for giving the appearance of aberration while it is, in fact, a smug parody of the language of pain: "Un poème qui est hors du coeur, hors de l'affre et du sanglot coeur, un poème qui n'a pas été *souffert*" (IX, 226).[14] Carroll is not only a coward for refusing to suffer his poem before writing it, but he is also a parasite of pain who feeds upon the pain of others. The case of "Jabberwocky" affects Artaud personally because he, like Carroll, uses invented language, and it is essential that he emphasize the difference between his poetry and that of the Victorian. Despite the apparent similarities noted by Henri Parisot, who suggested that Artaud translate "Jabberwocky," the two invented languages—Artaud's and Carroll's—are distinguished by the fact that Artaud's is made meaningful by pain while Carroll's is the nonsense of those who affect madness in order to display their learning. Artaud will continue to write in what he calls "la langue pure avec un sens hors grammatical" (IX, 185),[15] but he rebuffs any conjecture that he is engaging in word play. His is the meaning which comes from "affre cette vieille serve de peine, ce sexe de carcan enfoui qui sort ses vers de sa maladie" (IX, 185).[16]

Coleridge is another poet whose failure to write from the experience of pain attracts Artaud's attention. In "Coleridge le traître" (1948), Artaud calls him a traitor because he was given a chance to be a genuine poet, but he escaped suffering through visions offered by drugs. When he transforms the creative "mucus" into opium, Coleridge becomes vulnerable to the insidious snares of Christianity, little knowing that it is a more deceptive source of agony than the one from which he has suffered: "Je ne sais quel prêtre . . . l'a détourné vers la douleur affreuse que seule sa magie séculaire et préméditée a fabriquée, mais qui, en fait, n'avait pas existé."[17]

In his article on Coleridge, Artaud reveals two consequences of true poetry which are continuing preoccupations in his writing. The first is an etymologically based assertion that poetry will give rise to the world of cruelty which is depicted, as in Artaud's theater, in terms of blood:

> Car *après*, dit'poématique,' après viendra le temps
> du sang.
> Puisqu'*ema*, en grec, veut dire sang, et que po-ema
> doit vouloir dire:
> après
> le sang
> le sang aprés.
> Faisons d'abord *poème*, avec sang. (K, 93)[18]

A generative cycle emerges from poetry which contains this blood, for it gives rise to the shedding of new blood which, in turn, is to be transformed into poetry. The religious connotations of this chain of poetic martyrs suggest the influence of Aztec ritual on Artaud's theory of poetry.

The postulation of sexless birth, which appears frequently in Artaud's later texts, is supported by the second consequence of true, painful poetry. Again, the cycle of generation appears:

Oui, sous le tourniquet de la douleur, il y a un sang qui sort, une heure pour le caillot dégelé des ténèbres, et qui est, lui, ce véritable enfant sans sexe, né hors des parturitions limoneuses du sexe qui ne fut que la gorge et le clou d'un primitif étranglement. (K, 94)[19]

The blood clot which emerges from strangling pain is the poem, the pure, sexless product of a chaste conception. Because of its chastity, it enters into the bloody cycle of the "po-ema."

Although poets are, of course, Artaud's principal artistic landmarks when he seeks predecessors in pain, there are others who have made art of suffering. In his earlier texts, he displays an affinity for Paolo Uccello, for example, although the experiences of the subject in this case are apparently too remote to have direct repercussions in Artaud's later writing. Vincent Van Gogh, on the other hand, provides a familiar and popular example of the phenomenon of artistic creation in psychic and physical pain.

III   *Vincent Van Gogh*

Van Gogh, le suicidé de la société (*Van Gogh, Society's Suicide*), which is undoubtedly the most accessible of Artaud's late texts, was written in 1947 and appeared in December of the same year. A sympathetic but apparently apocryphal story spread by the art dealer Pierre Loeb relates that Artaud wrote this rather long text in only two days after a visit to a major Van Gogh exhibit at the Orangerie in Paris.[20] In fact, the writing of the text took place in several stages during the winter and early spring of 1947 after Artaud's visit to the Orangerie on February 2.

Artaud drew some of his material from Wilhelm Uhde's biography of Van Gogh and A. M. Rosset's critical study, as well as from the painter's letters to his brother Theo. While Artaud finds use and merit in these sources, he vehemently contests the speculations concerning Van Gogh's mental health which accompanied reviews of the Orangerie exhibition in the French press. As Thévenin notes, an important aspect of this text is the fact that it was dictated as well as written; it was produced as much for auditory as for visual effectiveness.

Two major divisions, an Introduction and the central text, "Le Suicidé de la société," are augmented by three postscripts, one placed after the introduction and two after the central text. It is unfortunate that the publication of *Van Gogh* in the *Oeuvres complètes* does not include reproductions of the paintings on which Artaud comments. However, most are easily called to mind by the reader; they include *La Nuit étoilée* (*Starry Night*), *Champs de blé* (*Wheat Fields*), and *Le Jardin de Daubigny* (*Daubigny's Garden*).

Artaud denies that Van Gogh was mad in any conventional sense and declares that society is so corrupt that an authentic "madman" ("aliéné") is a person of higher moral standing than his contemporaries. The "aliéné authentique" is both "un homme qui a préféré devenir fou, dans le sens où socialement on l'entend, que de forfaire à une certaine idée supérieure de l'honneur humain . . . un homme que la société n'a pas voulu entendre et qu'elle a voulu empêcher d'émettre d'insupportables vérités" (XIII, 17).[21] While society engages in the most disgusting sexual debauchery, this superior being is sublimely chaste; since that madness which is to be condemned derives from sexual sin, those who, like Van Gogh, are chaste (in the metaphysical sense) cannot be mad.

Artaud does not merely write an appreciation of Van Gogh; rather he sets out to rectify a general misunderstanding of the category of men to which he himself belongs:

On peut parler de la bonne santé mentale de Van Gogh qui, dans toute sa vie, ne s'est fait cuire qu'une main et n'a pas fait plus, pour le reste, que de se trancher une fois l'oreille gauche,
   dans un monde où on mange chaque jour du vagin cuit à la sauce verte ou du sexe de nouveau-né flagellé et mis en rage. (XIII, 13)[22]

For Artaud, the hypocrisy of a society which condemns innocent abberration while condoning and concealing truly monstrous behavior is an evil which must be denounced.

   The subtitle "suicidé de la société" certainly requires some explanation in light of its apparent paradox. Two aspects of this phrase recall earlier texts: the oxymoron (suicide is defined customarily by the absence of an external agent) echoes the subtitle of *Heliogabalus or The Crowned Anarchist*, while the fusion of internal and external impulse (suicide versus society) suggests some of the more disturbing turns of phrase of Artaud's "conversion" letters from Rodez and his identification of sensation and perception in parts of *Les Tarahumaras*.

   Indeed, like the Artaud of the Rodez letters, Van Gogh was the corporeal focus of warring forces:

Van Gogh n'est pas mort d'un état de délire propre, mais d'avoir été corporellement le champ d'un problème autour duquel, depuis les origines, se débat l'esprit inique de cette humanité.
   Celui de la prédominance de la chair sur l'esprit, ou du corps sur la chair, ou de l'esprit sur l'un et l'autre. (XIII, 20)[23]

Society will not tolerate a solution of the conflict between body and spirit because the one who has resolved it for himself automatically removes himself from the "general consciousness." When Van Gogh did so, this intangible power had its revenge by removing his supernatural consciousness and replacing it with a "possession" which is like possession by evil spirits. When *Van Gogh, le suicidé de la société* is read in light of Artaud's contemporary texts and the Rodez letters, it appears that this diagnosis is not metaphorical but literal, for the depiction of a bewitching or possession recurs frequently with regard to Artaud himself, as well as in his texts on Nerval and Lautréamont.

   Van Gogh's paintings are the subject of the central section, and

Artaud emphasizes the accuracy with which they depict the hidden workings of the cosmos:

> Cardés par le clou de Van Gogh,
> les paysages montrent leur chair hostile,
> la hargne de leurs replis éventrés,
> que l'on ne sait quelle force étrange est, d'autre
>   part, en train de métamorphoser. (XIII, 25)[24]

Hence, a Van Gogh exhibition ranks with other major revelations and prophecies as a historical date (XIII, 26), one which gives humanity a rare opportunity to perceive hidden truths. Obviously, a painting such as *The Crows*, which Van Gogh is said to have painted with the suicide bullet in his body, is a unique effort in the annals of art. But even in the most banal atmosphere, as in the famous picture of the artist's room, Van Gogh "déduit le Mythe des choses" ("deduces the Myth of things," XIII, 29), and Artaud warmly approves the artist's predilection for real, ordinary subject matter rather than myth or fable.

Artaud contends that no one since Van Gogh has found the "key to the fields," although it was sought by Symbolist and Surrealist alike. For an illustration of his heightened perception, Artaud turns to the painting entitled *The Crows*, in which he reads Van Gogh's fate. The apparent influence of the cardinal villain in his biography, Dr. Gachet, strikes a sympathetic chord: "Car c'est pourtant bien après une conversation avec le docteur Gachet que Van Gogh, comme si de rien n'était, est rentré dans sa chambre et s'est suicidé" (XIII, 37).[25] Doctors create illness—which Artaud consistently sees as an avoidable phenomenon not implicit in the human condition—so that they may live on it, and psychiatrists, feeding on and attempting to pervert the anguish of their patients, are the most reprehensible of all.

Because of his contact with Gachet, Van Gogh's brother Theo is implicated in the plot against Vincent, as is anyone who considers him mad. Theo also committed the unforgivable sin of procreation, which not only violates chastity but contributes to the birth of a son who Vincent felt replaced him in his brother's affections. In contrast with their petty concerns, the artist wishes to rearrange the world at his pleasure, to return creation to the melting pot.

Midway through the central section, at the climax of the text, are two excerpts and one complete text from Van Gogh's letters to Theo. Printed in italics, the three pieces appear as an artistic thesis and its illustration: an undated fragment describes drawing as a passage through an iron wall by the force of the will, which slowly and patiently undermines the barrier, while the second and third texts describe two successful efforts in this direction, *Café at Night* and *Daubigny's Garden*. Artaud praises the manner in which Van Gogh simply yet completely gives an account of the subject of his paintings as well as of their intended meaning. The brevity of these fragments heightens rather than restrains their impact: "Car le clou séparatif critère n'est pas une question d'ampleur ou de crampe, mais de simple force personnelle du poing" (XIII, 42).[26] This criterion also applies to Van Gogh's preference for the smallest, humblest subjects in his painting, as in his life. Each canvas is a pictorial elucidation of the "slow genesic nightmare" of human creation in a world which reaches beyond present appearance to the suffering which existed before birth.

While the introduction is principally negative, directed against the murderous society of psychiatrists, religious forces of all persuasions, and their accomplices (a group which includes most of humanity), the central portion of *Van Gogh* is a positive, lyric glorification of the painter and all he represents. On this side of the struggle are aligned the "aliénés authentiques" (Artaud, Nerval, and others) and the natural forces which Van Gogh depicted, along with the superior reality which he glimpsed but was not allowed to proclaim. In the purity of his colors, as in the clarity of his intent, Van Gogh was "le plus vraiment peintre de tous les peintres, le seul qui n'ait pas voulu dépasser la peinture," but for this very reason, "le seul qui, d'autre part, absolument le seul, ait absolument dépassé la peinture, l'acte inerte de représenter la nature pour, dans cette représentation exclusive de la nature, faire jaillir une force tournante, un élément arraché en pleine coeur" (XIII, 46).[27] The truth of painting, like that of the body, is not *beyond* but *within*.

Consequently, for Artaud, nature is like an enormous humanized corporeal entity which can be explained in terms of individual human experience. Unlike Gauguin, who sought to enlarge the living subject to exaggerated proportions, "Van Gogh pensait qu'il faut savoir déduire le mythe des choses les plus terre-à-terre de la vie" (XIII, 29)[28]—an approach which wins Artaud's approval. Reality properly interpreted is infinitely superior to any other possible worldview, whether of history, myth, or surreality. Van Gogh reaches depths unplumbed by overt occultism in both art and life by adhering strictly to the "motif," the matter of life and of painting.

Van Gogh's face rolls toward Artaud like the vision of a Juggernaut, red and explosive as in his self-portrait (XIII, 46, 49), bringing with it a return to the eschatological implications of his life and work. Again, Artaud defines his adversary, society, in opposition to its victims, which include himself: "Car ne sommes-nous pas tous, comme le pauvre Van Gogh lui-même, des suicidés de la société" (XIII, 50).[29] The early stages of human evolution, like the imminent apocalypse, are characterized by a state of unconscious war which is the result of ancient human sins. Van Gogh shows in his painting that he has passed beyond the world in which his own suns were the only joy. He accomplished this miraculous transplantation in the well-known incident when he sent his ear (which Artaud interprets as the physical representation of the soul) to a woman, "l'âme de son âme" ("the soul of his soul"), thereby putting a simultaneous end to the "sinister allusions" of the soul and to heterosexual eroticism.

But such an action is never left unpunished by society, and, in order to dethrone "king" Van Gogh, a new sin was fabricated, one which Artaud calls "la culture turque" ("Turkish culture," XIII, 51).[30] The violence of Van Gogh's life is legitimate—"qui ne sent pas la bombe cuite et le vertige comprimé n'est pas digne d'être vivant" (XIII, 53)[31]—but Turkish culture creates a facade of honesty behind which forces maneuver until they can steal Van Gogh's essence by killing him. The success of this stratagem is, however, merely apparent, for the peace created when the disruptive genius commits suicide is but a momentary pause in the perpetual war which is the real state of being in the world:

> Un jour la peinture de Van Gogh armée et de fièvre
> et de bonne santé
>   reviendra pour jeter en l'air la poussière d'un monde
>   en cage que son coeur ne pouvait plus supporter.
> (XIII, 54)[32]

The threat of apocalypse which looms in many of Artaud's writings from the mid-1930s onward is concretized in the form of an artists' revenge—one in which Artaud himself will participate.

The two concluding postscripts return to the question of Van Gogh's madness as it is directly related to Artaud's own experience of diagnosis and treatment. When he looks into Van Gogh's eyes in the self-portrait, Artaud sees a being who wanted to live for and in the infinite, whether as plenitude or as void. But the bestial masses were jealous of his relationship with the infinite and so conspired to force him into suicide. Van Gogh found that in death he might achieve union with the infinite; suicide was more appealing than the continuation of a life which he felt to be burdensome to himself and others. When his brother became a father and when Gachet reprimanded him for his delirium, he had had enough—Artaud says that he would feel the same impulse—and a knot of blood in his throat killed him. Again, strangulation (like Nerval's hanging) and not the gunshot wound of which Van Gogh actually died is the strongest image of suicide for Artaud, and one which predicts his own end.

As narrator of *Van Gogh*, Artaud is a survivor who shares a fearful experience with his subject. In the final postscript, he returns to a topic familiar from his *Lettres de Rodez:* terrible natural cataclysms and scenes of human debauchery took place between February and May of 1946 and have been effaced from the common memory. These orgiastic rituals sprang from an overwhelming hatred like that which killed Van Gogh, but they were directed against Artaud himself, who survived miraculously.

As in the case of *Héliogabale*, the distance between subject and object is less important in *Van Gogh* than their identity, and it is from this conjunction of artistic essences that the life of Van Gogh, like that of Nerval, draws its ultimate value and Artaud's message its urgency.

When he emerged from incarceration in institutions, Artaud became less concerned with the fate of historical forebears than with his own place in the world. In his final texts, all external reality recedes before the primacy of his own life experience as a pattern for the structure of reality.

CHAPTER 7

Torture and Triumph

EXPLORATION of the lives of other artists led Artaud away from the belief that an organized set of religious practices could save either himself or the world from suffering and destruction. In his last texts, he sets forth his personal experience, just as he used that of Van Gogh, Nerval and others, as the exemplary pattern for the workings of the world. Most important, he evaluates every phenomenon according to strictly physical criteria and criticizes the constitution of the human body itself. In order to remake the world in the shape of his body, he finds that he must first refashion his anatomy so as to protect it from the depredations of the unreformed environment in which it exists.

Because it is impossible to account for all the poems and fragments of these last years in this study,[1] the focus of this chapter will be limited to three well-defined texts: *Artaud le Mômo (Artaud the Mômo)*, *Ci-gît (Here Lies)*, and *Pour en finir avec le jugement de dieu (To Have Done with God's Judgment)*. Each is a poem, augmented by a group of notes, fragments, and drafts which reinforces its integral identity. On the other hand, the unity of the texts varies: while *Artaud le Mômo* is readily perceived as a whole, the unity of *Pour en finir avec le jugement de dieu* is circumstantial, not internal, and *Ci-gît* is preceded by *La Culture indienne*, a different text which was published with the longer poem.

Very little of Artaud's writing lends itself to critical analysis, and these final texts are the most difficult to read in any sense. Their identity is oral and physical as well as scriptorial, and any written account of their content is inadequate. On the other hand, attempts to speak of Artaud in his own tongue lose the reader entirely by rendering the texts more opaque than they are originally.[2] While Artaud's writing defies paraphrasing, much less rational explanation, it can in some measure be discussed, for Artaud is not unapproachable, and to dismiss him as such is to ignore his position entirely.

I *Artaud the Mômo*

"Artaud the Mômo," the persona who speaks in the 1947 texts of *Artaud le Mômo*, is the Artaud whose existence is, in the strongest sense, the life of his works, the flesh of his words (*mots-mots*). The word "Mômo" suggests "môme," the colloquial word "brat," and refers the reader back to childhood, one of the major preoccupations of this and other texts of the period. *Mômo* is the reverse of *om-om*, a doubling of the Hindu chanting syllable which Artaud ridicules on several occasions (usually spelling it *aum*), often making it a pun for *homme (man)* as in the title *L'Aume et l'Arve*.[3]

There are five poems in *Artaud le Mômo*, and they are strongly united by theme, language (or rather, languages), and tone. Each represents an attempt to regain control over an existence which has long been the puppet of legal, psychoanalytical and technological intervention. Characteristically, Artaud must possess himself absolutely from the outset, as well as in the here and now. Consequently, the expulsion of an alien influence begins with the components of being: flesh and spirit. Spirit, the soul, all that which is intangible or idea, is an invasion of the fleshly self through the orifices of the body. Control of one's life begins with the literal and philosophical expulsion of all ethereal demons.

The idea of extinguishing ideas contains an inherent contradiction. Artaud's language aims to circumvent the problem by its violence and materiality (when it is referential) and by the use of neologisms and invented language. Hence, "Le Retour d'Artaud le Mômo" ("The Return of Artaud the Mômo") begins:

> L'esprit ancré
> vissé en moi
> par la poussé
> psycho-lubrique
> de ciel
> est celui qui pense
> toute tentation
> tout désir
> toute inhibition.
>
> o dedi
> a dada orzoura
> o dou zoura
> a dada skizi. (XIII, 13)[4]

One maleficent intangible, the spirit, is caused by another, heaven. Both are linked with the demon of sexuality, and both are expressed in the form of an incantation. The close interweaving of repeated syllables suggests meanings but cannot be translated. "Dada," for example, recalls Dadaism, while the ending "-ra" suggests a future tense. Only the final word of this brief passage in invented language is clear: *skizi* is linked with schizophrenia. The nature of this connection and its relation to the context are issues to be resolved by each reader.

However, resolution of the relationship between body and spirit alone does not suffice. The second problem is the individual's control over the circumstances of his entrance into the world. The "facts of life" are not facts at all to Artaud, and he denies vehemently and repeatedly that he was born in the customary fashion. Two examples from this period illustrate his point of view. In a letter dated August 9, 1946, he writes:

> J'aurai cinquante ans le 4 septembre prochain, ce qui ne veut pas dire que je sois né à Marseille le 4 septembre 1896 comme le porte mon état civil,
>
> mais je me souviens d'y être passé une certaine nuit en effet à l'heure de patron-minet.
>
> Je me souviens d'y avoi fait moi-même mon *incarnation* cette nuit-là, au lieu de l'avoir reçue d'un père et d'une mère. (XIII, 227)[5]

Writing to Peter Watson two weeks earlier, he explains that he chose to be a man rather than a woman because the female has the deplorable association of holes and *anima*, which suggests *âme*, the immaterial soul. Likewise, the title "L'Exécration du père-mère" ("Execration of the Father-Mother") in *Artaud le Mômo* clarifies Artaud's intention, even if the text does not.

Like birth, death should be a matter of choice, not an inevitability. Artaud repeatedly insists, from *Les Nouvelles Révélations de l'Etre* on, that death has been introduced into the world by eroticism and black magic. Again in the letter to Peter Watson, he states that death is useless and does not really exist, and he reinforces this assertion with an account of a personal experience of death on four occasions: in Marseilles, Lyons, Mexico, and Rodez. In each instance, his mind left his body and hovered over it, but it eventually returned of its own volition (XII, 232).

In contrast with this ultimate control over life and death, Artaud vilifies the state of the "unconditioned," which occurs beyond the

will of individual physical being. "Insulte à l'inconditionné" ("Insult
to the Unconditioned") lists effects of the "rats" of this uncontrolled
force from which Artaud himself has suffered:

> interférence de l'action,
> le transfert par déportation,
> le rétablissement hors coupure,
> la coupure des colmatations;
> l'assise enfin
> dans le non-hors. (XII, 30)[6]

These and other consequences are isomorphic in that each is the
interruption of a congested or established state of being: action,
travel, corporeal unity, clogging. The subject is displaced into a
different context when action is impeded, the voyager deported, the
body excised, or the clogging opened. The rats can be expelled only
in the filth of verbal abuse.

The unconditioned or the conditionless ("sans-condition") is an
externality which influences the life of the subject or which forces its
way into the individual consciousness. In "Aliénation et magie noire"
("Alienation and Black Magic"), Artaud gives voice to yet another
verbal assault which aims to exterminate these occult forces which
enslave the inmate of insane asylums. The culprits in this case are not
the oriental necromancers of the *Lettres de Rodez* but the doctors in
these institutions:

> ce n'est pas seulement que les médecins favorisent
> la magie par leurs thérapeutiques intempestives et
> hybrides,
> c'est qu'ils en font.
>
> S'il n'y avait pas eu de médecins
> il n'y aurait jamais eu de malades. (XII, 57)[7]

Since illness is a forthright manifestation of the effects of the non-self
on the self, this reasoning leads Artaud to place the medical profes-
sion, especially psychiatry, among the agents of death and the
spoliation of the self. The state to which medicine reduces its victims
through shock treatments leaves them susceptible to the sinister
force of Bardo (roughly, the Tibetan version of the spirit of death); no
longer conscious of their own identity, they become like the dead.

This artificially created death is necessary to the continuation of manipulations by the black magicians who are disguised as healers.

Finally, then, the madness with which Artaud was branded throughout this institutional period is both a birth and a death in that it is a contingent, unnatural state imposed on him by God and His collaborators. The text ends with two pages designed to reduce "god" to an abject state, as well as to annul the special value given to words (XIII, 61). The active, living nature of the texts is also emphasized in these pages, which are so positioned that they protect the book from "all the swarming of Bardo" which threatens it. The first two pages contain a poem which is printed in italics and emphasizes the language of Bardo itself; again, its function is to cast into doubt the existence of the self:

> *Tu n'es plus là*
> *mais rien ne te quitte.*
> *tu as tout conservé*
> *sauf toi-même*
> *et que t'importe puisque*
> *le monde*
> *est là.*
>
> *Le*
> *monde,*
> *mais ce n'est plus moi.*
> *Et que t'importe*
> *dit le Bardo*
> *c'est moi.* (XII, 64)[8]

The world, the Bardo, God, death, birth, the unconditioned, are threats to the individual's existence because they suggest that it is not self-contained, self-controlled, and all powerful.

Yet, the final tone of *Artaud le Mômo* is not omniscient but rather puzzled, querulous, and obscure. In a "Post-Scriptum," Artaud complains that under the influence of shock treatments he met dead people who were emitted by the same forces described in the *Bardo Todol* (the Tibetan Book of the Dead). His last word is simply the question "Why," which would seem to have been answered by the entire text. In this manner, Artaud urges upon his reader a repetition of his own words and assures himself of some control over the pullulating realm of non-self. The fate of the text, like that of the individual, must be controlled as much as possible.

II *To Make a New Body*

The first drafts of both *La Culture indienne (Indian Culture)* and *Ci-gît (Here lies)* were written at one sitting on November 25, 1946. A laborious process of polishing and transcription, during which Artaud dictated the text to Paule Thévenin, brought both poems to the final state.[9]

Although the two poems have a great deal in common, they are separate texts. The first is relatively brief (four pages in the Gallimard edition) and appears without major internal breaks, while the second (twenty-three pages) contains sixteen distinct sections and is printed in the wide variety of styles found in conventional typography; all lower or upper case, boldface, italics, liberal use of white space, and numerals. Four sections of *Ci-gît* have headings: a "commentary," two "morals," and a "conclusion."

On first reading, the contents of *La Culture indienne* seem to have little to do with its title. There are, in fact, many more direct references to Indian culture in *Ci-gît* than in the opening poem. The first line, "Je suis venu au Mexique prendre contact avec la Terre Rouge" ("I came to Mexico to make contact with the Red Land," XII, 71), suggests a harking back to the subject matter of *Les Tarahumaras*. But the poem immediately deserts this geographical locus in favor of a more general series of concerns: birth, Christianity, and the nature of human existence. What has happened to Indian culture? A clue appears in lines 10–12:

> le trou à creux, l'âcre trou creux, où bout le cycle
>   des poux rouges
> cycle des poux solaires rouges
> tout blancs dans le lacis des veines de l'un deux.
>
> (XII, 71)[10]

The solar cult of the Mexicans has been transformed into the verminous (*poux*) circulation of red/white blood cells, which are like miniature suns in the veins of "the one two."

There are striking similarities between this poem and Artaud's *Héliogabale*. In the prose text, the protagonist overcame the dualities of war between red and white, birth out of blood and sperm, and masculine and feminine principles in his extraordinary reign. *La Culture indienne* denounces the same binary nature of human existence: "Pourquoi deux d'eux / et pourquoi de DEUX?"; "et ça veut dire que la guerre / remplacera le père-mère" (XII, 72–73).[11] Because of this persistent division into "the one two," Artaud was unable to yield fully to "la peste nourricière / de la Terre Rouge" ("the nutritive plague / of the Red Land," XII, 73). Reminiscent of the inadequate realization of theater in the mid-1930s, the failure of the mission to Mexico is blamed on the dual nature of the human condition. The problem of conception and parturition is also a major concern of *Ci-gît*.

Two more evils have entered human life because of the dual human condition. The first is Christianity, for Jesus Christ is a sinister interloper between the self (*ji* is a variant of "je") and its expression (*cri*, a cry) when he appears in the degraded, deformed, but recognizable shape of a *jiji-cricri* (also written *jizo-cri*):

> interlope entre ji et cri
> contracté en
>   jiji-cricri. (XII, 72)[12]

When the problem of Jesus returns in *Ci-gît*, it is resolved by the identification of Artaud himself as a source of Christian mythology. First, it is a product of his suffering, as are his own parents:

> C'est ainsi qu'on
> tira de moi
> papa et maman
> et la friture de ji en
> Cri
>
> . . . .
> qui donna vie
> à Jizo-cri. (XII, 87)[13]

But, as we learn later, "Jizo-cri" never really had any existence at all. Like the "demiurge" of *Artaud le Mômo*, his being is a fraud:

> Ne voit-on pas que le gendre faux
> c'est jizi-cri
> déjà connu au Mexique
> bien avant sa fuite à Jérusalem sur un âne,
> et le crucifiement d'Artaud au Golgotha
> Artaud
> qui savait bien qu'il n'y a pas d'esprit
> mais un corps. (XII, 94)[14]

Artaud's self-identification as the true presence at Calvary has already appeared in the contexts of *Les Tarahumaras* and the Rodez letters. For him, then, the archetypal victim is not Jesus, who was contaminated by the Holy Spirit, but himself, the latest avatar in the line of suffering persecuted artists. Consequently he arrogates to himself the right to found a new faith which will combat and overcome the insidious influence of Christianity.

According *to Ci-gît*, Artaud was crucified because he knew that existence is purely physical. The nature of this corporeal being is the third major concern of both *La Culture indienne* and *Ci-gît*. Like birth and Christianity, it is an area of combat for two opposing principles: plenitude, which finds its fullest expression in bone, and nothingness, as exemplified by the threatening presence of orifices in the bodily whole. This duality, and the intermediate degrees of solidity and softness which make up the body, are the single most consistent preoccupations of *Ci-gît*. In the prefatory poem, they are present in the suggestion of a hierarchy among the parts of the body. The miniature suns circulating in the veins are inferior to the "vieille jambe ossuaire gangrène/où mûrit un bouclier d'os" ("old charnelhouse gangrene limb/where a shield of bone ripens," XII, 72); the extremities, which are primarily solid matter, are valued over the viscera, with its independent organs and orifices.

The concluding passage of *La Culture indienne* returns to the opposition of round and straight which is found in the original denunciation of cycles. The "round" of the heavens invades the body, which is filled with emptiness, so that the void outside the body, rather than swallowing up physical existence, is subsumed by the rigidity of muscle and bone, "quand on est droit de tout son long" ("when one is straight for his whole length," XII, 74). Although the orifice is round, its pernicious openness is overcome if the body is adequately disciplined.

Besides introducing the major subjects of *Ci-gît*, *La Culture indienne* displays a formal intricacy which is characteristic of Artaud's late poems. There are many instances of strong assonance, as in the line "le trou à creux, l'âcre trou rouge, où bout le cycle des poux rouges" (XII, 71), in which the choice of words and their arrangement are dictated by sound as much as by meaning. Some series of verses share a common length, most frequently octosyllabic, while others contain marked internal rhythms. These intermittent uses of intentional versification also appear in *Ci-gît*, but the language of the longer poem is much further from common usage than that of *La Culture indienne*.

The title *Ci-gît* creates an enigma: who lies here, who is dead? Is it Artaud himself, reduced by the depredations of sinister beings and by his terrible sufferings to the state of a cadaver? Or is God dead, or perhaps Jesus? We are unlikely to learn from the poem for as it states, "Tout vrai langage/est incompréhensible" ("All true language/is incomprehensible," XII, 95).

Ci-gît is designed to be read aloud, like most of Artaud's later poetry. There are even a few directions for its performance, such as "ceci chuchoté" ("this whispered," XII, 90). The language of the poem, while not entirely opaque, grows more distant from general usage insofar as it fulfills Artaud's criteria for truth. Phoneticized spelling (*DIZJE* for *dis-je*, *lomonculus* for *l'homonculus*), neologisms (*falzourchte, parpougnète*), and invented language appear frequently, along with passages which appear to be referential or common usage but leave the reader puzzled. A sequence such as the following, with its incantatory quality, gains meaning by its physical force rather than through the use of verbal form:

> Car je fus Inca mais pas roi
> **kilzi**
> **trakilizi**
> **faildor**
> **bara bama**
> **baraba**
> **mince**
>
> etretili
> TILI
> te pince
> dans la *falzourchte*
> de tout or,
> dans la déroute
> de ton corps. (XII, 81–82)[15]

Syllabic fragments tantalize the reader who recites the invented-language passage: "qu'ils y" or "qu'il s'y," "il dort," "barra," and "Barrabbas," among others. The final word in boldface is standard French—"thin," or a mild expletive in popular usage. In the context of the "Inca," the passage might relate a conquest and exploitation by invaders, especially when the references to gold and a rout are included. But no interpretation is satisfactory, and the passage remains intact.

On the other hand, the famous opening section is declamatory and clear in its refutation of normal birth and recall of *Artaud le Mômo*:

> Moi, Antonin Artaud, je suis mon fils, mon père, ma mère et moi;
> niveleur du périple imbécile où s'enferre l'engendrement
> le périple papa-maman
>   et l'enfant. (XII, 77)[16]

Giving birth to himself, Artaud is freed of the implications of sexual parturition and conception. Birth is but an "impossible hole" invented by an evil spirit to turn us against our bodies. The second section adds another facet to this denunciation of the commonly accepted human condition. A "being" born of heaven, accursed, and yet chosen by a maleficent god, is the bane of the human existence of another child, Artaud himself. His own birth is described as coming from the fingerless arm of a regicide Inca.

Ensuing sections describe Artaud's battles with "les êtres," which usurp his life, and his attempts to overpower them with his "myrmidons." The poem entitled "commentaire" enumerates the evils visited upon his body by his enemies: he was made to eat poisonous eggs and his body was emptied of matter. Two of the numbered aggressions performed by "les saligauds" ("the bums") are recounted partly in invented-language syllables, while others appear in standard French. The following page contains a single statement: "ET ILS, ONT TOUS FOUTU LE CAMP" ("AND THEY HAVE ALL CLEARED OUT"), and the "ils" apparently refers to the "beings" of the preceding sections. Hence, the villains are no longer around to be punished, and they must be captured by the force of incantation and exorcism.

What is the result of this long and painful torture? Although a borer ("vrille") remains to torment him, Artaud has succeeded in creating the solidity of bone out of the volcanic ash ("tuff") left by his spoliation. Once he has become entirely bone, he can begin to create on his own. The two "morals" repeat the essential nature of this new cultural foundation: "Ne te fatigue jamais plus qu'il ne faut, quitte à fonder une culture sur la fatigue de tes os"; "os par os/l'égalisation sempiternelle revint" (XII, 97 and 98).[17]

The conclusion restates the position of "moi, simple/Antonin Artaud" with regard to the father and mother, God, Jesus, or any other being which attempts to take his life away. He simply does not believe in them and therefore renders himself invulnerable to their attacks. The final rejection is that of time itself, for his new, deathless existence is beyond time:

> comme si le temps
> n'était pas frite
> n'était pas cette cuite frite
> de tous les effrités
> du seuil,
> réembarqués dans leur cerceuil. (XII, 100)[18]

The new body cannot be changed ("cooked") by time, cannot "crumble," cannot be buried in a coffin. "Here lies," then, an emptiness in which the defiant Artaud refuses to be buried.

III *God: The Ultimate Adversary*

Artaud's last book-length work, *Pour en finir avec le jugement de dieu (To Have Done with God's Judgment)*[19] is a summation of his polemical and metaphysical stance and of his technical explorations in theater. Its execution was yet another agonizingly frustrating experience, and the consequence exhaustion and despair may well have contributed to his death. The story of the rejection of Artaud's radio performance of the *Judgment* by the administration of the French radio network differs from Artaud's earlier abortive projects insofar as the performance had been solicited and its cancellation was strongly protested by a number of powerful figures. But the pattern of hope, effort, and failure remains to characterize Artaud's interaction with his potential audience.

The performance was banned because the text of *To Have Done with God's Judgment* was found to be potentially offensive to Americans. The poems advocate extermination of the spiritual, the ideal, and chance in favor of a controllable, physical reality. This new order can only be installed through the creation of an entirely new language. It must have two essential qualities: personal specificity (it is not borrowed from the common speech of God in the masses) and corporeality (it communicates with the entire body, not merely with the senses of sight and hearing). Artaud's later poems must be heard and felt in their rhythmic wholeness or their meaning is annulled. The simultaneous presence of both qualities would compensate for the well-known hazards which accompany attempts to communicate in an idiolect (personal language), for lacunae which might arise in interpretation would be filled with meaning conveyed by the physical sensations of rhythm and sound. Hence, a converging set of over-determinations reinforces the inevitable underdetermination of such a highly individualized language. Insofar as thought is structured and expressed in language, Artaud's incantatory syllables cannot be "translated" into a parallel linguistic order; indeed, to do so would deny the very qualities for which he values them. Rather, they—and much of the apparently normal, referential language in these poems—are the raw fruits of pain, of choking breath, of the realm of physical being which verbalism fails to touch.

Artaud aims to transform the very state of being of the readers and listeners by moving them physically. Despite his urgent dedication to this end, he does not rely solely upon the creation of a language capable of action. The polemic content of *Judgment* is clearly and bluntly stated in a language which seeks its effectiveness in the horror of its meaning rather than in the strangeness of its form. It is a series of six poems, one of which is the conclusion, on a familiar variety of topics.

The focus of the first two texts is the Western world: the warmon-gering depravity of the United States is contrasted with the purifying rituals of the Tarahumaras. The account of American crimes is likely to cause physical revulsion even in those untouched by incantation. According to Artaud, sperm is taken from American boys when they enter primary school in order to ensure by means of artificial insemi-nation that the American population will remain sufficiently large to cover the earth with an array of synthetic products designed to replace and extinguish natural life. Opposed to this rational, positivis-tic approach to the world, the rite of the black sun of the Tarahumaras installs the reign of unreason and fragmentation: "crève la croix afin que les espaces de l'espace ne puissent plus jamais se rencontrer ni se croiser" (XIII, 74).[20] "Tutuguri," as this text is entitled, places the familiar Tarahumara material in a new context as part of the work of summation which characterizes the verbal content of *Judgment*.

If reason and orientation in space are abolished, what remains to give humanity an index of its being in the world? The answer is clear in the title of the next section, "Recherche de la fécalité" ("Search for Fecality"). Man has a clear choice; to be or not to be; that is, to defecate or not to defecate. But to go beyond mere existence into life, man must be prepared to avoid the easy choice of being "meat," and to go into the hardness of bone. This is what humanity has never been

willing to do: only Artaud can see the consequences of valuing the
"infini dehors" ("infinite without"), the solid structure of unyielding
bone, over the "infime dedans" ("infinitesimal within"), which is
vulnerable, soft, and spiritual. The lesson of *Ci-gît* is repeated in a
new context in this final poem.

God's judgment makes us mortal, unclean creatures, but those
who (unlike the fraudulent Jesus Christ) have been truly crucified
know that God does not exist in the reality of feces and bone. The
Roman Catholic Mass, which purports to give communicants his
transsubstantiated bone, is a pernicious, erotic fraud: "Je renie le
baptême et la messe" ("I repudiate baptism and the mass," XIII, 86).
Revolt against the judgment of God is, therefore, an attempt to end
the power of the invisible over the visible, the unreal over the real.

But God is not the only invisible force which rules Artaud's life. In
"La question se pose de . . ." ("The Question Is Asked"), consciousness and "l'idée" (the idea) are added to the list of concepts which
must be replaced by realities. Artaud's body and his pain are the only
true presences. He will tolerate interrogation and challenges (an
apparent allusion to the psychiatrists who have examined him), but
he bridles at anything which impinges upon his body:

> C'est qu'on me pressait
> jusqu'à mon corps
> et jusqu'au corps
> et c'est alors
> que j'ai tout fait éclater
> parce qu'à mon corps
> on ne touche jamais. (XIII, 97)[21]

This climactic moment of *Judgment* affirms that the body is Artaud's
last line of defense.

The conclusion is presented in the form of a dialogue between
Artaud and a hypothetical antagonistic interviewer who repeatedly
interjects the comment that Artaud is mad. First the voice of Artaud
incorporates the principle of cruelty into the material presented
earlier with regard to American imperialism. While the Indian had a
civilization based on cruelty in the elimination of God and "le hasard
bestial de l'animalité inconsciente humaine," ("the bestial chance of
unconscious human animality," XIII, 102), Americans have refashioned God in microbes with which the atomic bomb is made. The
second half of the conclusion proposes a radical solution to this

growing threat: to make man go through an "autopsy" which would refashion his anatomy. Only when organs, including the male member, are eliminated, will man be truly free, restored to wholeness beyond the power of God.

"Le Théâtre de la cruauté," written in 1947, was to have been part of the abortive radio performance, but it was cut because of the limited time available.[22] The text continues both the ideas and the form of *Judgment* with the addition of a redefinition of the Theater of Cruelty in light of the new worldview proposed in the preceding text. The dance and song of true theater are the only means by which the human anatomy can be diverted from the debauched, disease-ridden ends to which it has been sacrificed. The villains here are not Americans but "god" and Satan working through rituals performed on distant mountains by skirted priests whose torture of Artaud dates from the Rodez period. Thus despite his rejection of organized religion, Artaud continues to refer to the ritual of Christianity as well as that of other cults, because their wrongdoings must be denounced before the public in order to undermine their influence.

Apart from his reaffirmation of belief in the malevolent creatures who dance out his pain and physical deterioration, the most important foundation for Artaud's projected reconstruction of the human body lies in his exclusive adherence to the tangible:

> il n'y a rien d'existant et de réel
> que la vie physique extérieure
> et que tout ce qui la fuit et s'en détourne
> n'est que les limbes du monde des démons. (XIII, 110)[23]

The body is confronted with the insurmountable problem of its susceptibility to disease and death, and its hunger becomes crystallized, beyond alimentary or sexual appetite, in the desire for action. The site of this superhunger is the colon and its portal the anus; when it becomes manifest in the world, it is what Artaud calls KHA KHA. The spelling allows a double meaning to be conveyed: at once the childish word for excrement *(caca)* and the Egyptian word for the breath which is the living double of the dead body. In breath and feces, then, the Theater of Cruelty comes into the world in order to wipe out spirituality, eroticism, disease, and death—all of which are, again, the evil work of "god"'s judgment in the world. God does not exist in the sense that Artaud gives to existence, but his influence has effects in the world of man.

The concluding postscript to "Le Théâtre de la cruauté" is Artaud's final and most forceful statement of the position he takes in the world, and it deserves to be quoted in full:

> Qui suis-je?
> D'où je viens?
> Je suis Antonin Artaud
> et que je le dise
> comme je sais le dire
> immédiatement
> vous verrez mon corps actuel
> voler en éclats
> et se ramasser
> sous dix mille aspects
> notoires
> un corps neuf
> où vous ne pourrez
> plus jamais
> m'oublier. (XIII, 118)[24]

Two decades after his death, the "ten thousand ways" of Artaud's posthumous body remain with us, his readers.

CHAPTER 8

Conclusion

T HE experience of pain is central to Artaud's writing throughout his adult life. Suffering, illness, and torture are fundamental to his view of himself and of the world when he separates himself from literary traditions in his correspondence with Jacques Rivière: "Je souffre d'une effroyable maladie de l'esprit" (I, 20).[1] In the migrating network of sensation and anesthesia which characterizes Artaud's somatic experience, it is pain which provides a focus of feeling and which raises the inevitable question of the reason behind human suffering. Artaud writes from the conviction that his pain is a meaningful experience with both metaphysical and corporeal repercussions, especially during and after his nine years as an inmate in mental institutions. When he considers the work of other writers, he finds that there is no true meaning without pain. As for himself: "Je suis un homme qui a beaucoup souffert, et à ce titre j'ai le *droit* de parler" (I, 28).[2]

Artaud's repeated insistence upon the unity of his personal experience and his writing means that his life has the qualities of a text. Indeed, the inscribed character of his life is all the more striking in view of the vast number of letters in which he transforms the immediate but incommunicable experience of pain into text, asking the reader to diagnose, define, systematize, and comprehend the experience which he can but circumscribe in the inadequate palimpsest of written language. Artaud's writing is characterized by rupture and fragmentation; while it alternately commands and rejects interpretation, it never takes the classical stance of neutrality or transparency in the world.

In his analysis of the topic of Artaud's pain, Maurice Blanchot leaves his reader with a question: "Est-ce que l'extrême pensée et l'extrême souffrance ouvriraient le même horizon? Est-ce que souffrir serait, finalement, penser?"[3] Blanchot's question can be an-

swered in the affirmative through a study of the vital function of pain
in Artaud's writings. Not only does suffering provide a mode of
apprehending the world which displaces rational thought, but meaningful thought is also the product of suffering. [4]

Although confusion arises in Artaud's letters to Rivière when
mental and physical pain are equated, this psycho-physiological
interaction is not mere vacillation: it is the very nature of pain as it is
perceived by its most learned students. [5] Artaud's suffering from a
terrible illness is magnified by his feeling that the physical effects of
the disease generate distinct sensations: "Une électricité imprévue et
soudaine" or "ces tornades profondes" (I, 41–42). [6] Others may
display the same outward signs of distress as Artaud, but whereas
they retain their physical well-being, he is tortured. Writing in
response to Rivière's suggestion that Artaud's problems resemble
those of Tzara, Breton, or Reverdy, he explains: "Il n'en reste pas
moins qu'ils ne souffrent pas et que je souffre, non pas seulement
dans l'esprit, mais dans la chair et dans mon âme de tous les jours" (I,
39). [7] For Artaud himself, his suffering is the distinctive mark of his
being in the world.

Artaud is not alone in the aristocracy of pain, for all true artists
suffer. Art as the product of suffering in the most general sense recalls
the dictum in the preface to Le Théâtre et son double that one must be
like a martyr at the stake signaling through the flames. Certainly
Artaud himself fulfills this qualification with his "sensibilité
d'écorché" ("sensitivity of one who is burned," V, 239), which infuses
every text. He describes his own work as a place where, instead of
saying or doing, "on souffre" ("one suffers," XII, 236). In the preamble to the publication of his Oeuvres complètes, he urges that his texts
be understood in light of his pain: "Les paroles sont un limon qu'on
n'éclaire pas du côté de l'être mais du côté de son angoisse" (I, 11). [8]
Likewise, the essay "Sur le théâtre balinais" ("On Balinese Theater")
repeats the idea that pain is essential to meaningful expression and
adds that it is the role of poetry to include the dimension of anguish
(IV, 76).

In early texts, Artaud's description of his pain is more explicitly
physical. The "Description d'un état physique" ("Description of a
Physical State") in L'Ombilic des limbes is a catalogue of sensations
which share the quality of pain: "brûlure" ("burning"), "muscles
tordus" ("twisted muscles"), "brisante douleur" ("breaking pain"),
"engourdissement douleureux" ("painful swelling"). These sensations are collected in groups which account for diverse clusters of pain

over the whole body. Even at this early date, Artaud has turned to narcotics as a means to counterattack pain. His "Lettre à Monsieur le législateur de la loi sur les stupéfiantes" ("Letter to the Legislator of the Law on Narcotics"), which is also included in *L'Ombilic des limbes*, expresses his philosophy of pain, as well as of painkillers: "Je suis maître de ma douleur. Tout homme est juge, et juge exclusif, de la quantité de douleur physique, ou encore de vacuité mentale qu'il peut honnêtement supporter" (I, 67).[9] Again, as in the letter to Rivière, physical and mental distress are intrinsically linked, and opium, Artaud's drug of choice at this time, is effective in combatting both varieties of anguish. *Le Pèse-nerfs (The Nerve Scale)* continues the pattern of frequent allusions to pain. Artaud's entire being is identified with his illness; he is no more and no less than a sick man: "Que mon mal ait reculé ou avancé, la question pour moi n'est pas là, elle est dans ma douleur" (I, 91).[10]

The enumeration of symptoms is even more frequent in Artaud's letters than in his poetry, especially since a large portion of his correspondence is addressed to doctors and their wives. In the 1920s and early 1930s, when he was under the care of the sympathetic doctors Toulouse and Allendy, Artaud hoped for a physical diagnosis which would lead to the alleviation of his pain and eventually to a cure. But he soon lost faith in scientific medicine—neither Allendy nor Toulouse practiced empirical medicine—and he sought help at the hands of a thaumaturgist, to whom he recounted his litany of suffering and added that he feared general paralysis (IS, 103–104). As early as 1921, he is haunted by the idea that pain might be an enduring part of his life: in a letter to Génica Athanasiou, he writes of having the impression that it is "something IRREMEDIABLE."[11]

In Artaud's later texts, while pain is still the fundamental ground of his being, it is always accompanied by an explanation of its origin:

> mais il y a une chose
> qui est quelque chose
> une seule chose
> qui soit quelque chose
> et que je sens
> à ce que ça veut SORTIR:
> la présence
> de ma douleur
> de corps. (XIII, 95–96)[12]

Although Artaud had long since given up hope of a cure, he ceased to view his pain as a negative quality against which he had to struggle. His pain becomes his reality.

In a spirit of bravura, Artaud writes to Rivière: "J'ai choisi le domaine de la douleur et de l'ombre, comme d'autres celui du rayonnement et de l'entassement de la matière" (I, 113).[13] Only when pain is valued as a genuine part of experience can knowledge be acquired, understanding which is inaccessible to the normal individual. Pain is greater than well-being: "L'idée de la souffrance est plus forte que l'idée de la guérison, l'idée de la vie" (LG, p. 118).[14] Knowledge is first of all knowledge of pain, and Artaud links the words "chair" ("flesh"), "sensibilité" ("sensitivity"), and "connaissance" ("knowledge") with the "appropriation" of his pain in a causal chain (I, 237). Not only will Artaud attempt to think his pain away,[15] but he will also direct his pain-heightened consciousness to metaphysical areas which are ignored by rational thought.

Such an approach may seem paradoxical in view of Artaud's lifelong emphasis on the unique qualities of the body and the limitation of his interest to whatever influences his flesh (I, 109). But it is the association of pain with metaphysics which leads directly to his Theater of Cruelty: "Dans l'état de dégénérescence où nous sommes, c'est par la peau qu'on fera rentrer la métaphysique dans l'esprit" (IV, 118).[16] Artaud's discovery of cruelty as a motivating principle of the universe, a perpetual conflict in which life-or-death struggles are going on at every moment, elicits descriptions which are remarkably like those of his own pain. The plague described in "Le Théâtre et la peste" ("Theater and the Plague") is, consequently, "comme une douleur qui, à mesure qu'elle croît en intensité et qu'elle s'enfonce, multiplie ses avenues et ses richesses dans tous les cercles de la sensibilité" (IV, 28).[17] Not only does cruelty awaken the brutalized consciousness, but consciousness gives rise to further pain: the color of blood is the very signal of consciousness in life (IV, 121).

Outside the theater, the most explicit account of consciousness and its derivation from pain appears in "Je n'ai jamais rien étudié . . ." ("I have never studied anything . . .").[18] Hounded by "Mr colique, Mr crampe, Mr nausée, Mr vertige, Mr fessée, Mr calottes," a painful, personified spectrum reminiscent of "Description d'un état physique," the scandalized soul of a mistreated child comes to awareness and individuality. The infant consciousness, ill-at-ease in physical being, develops into a paradoxical state, "où l'être n'est bien que dans le mal de l'être."[19] Pain is a noble stigma which characterizes the sufferer as a superior being who exists on a plane different from normal humanity, which is resigned to mediocrity. Hence, Artaud can end this text on a triumphant note: "Bénie soit toute maladie, car la maladie sonde l'être, et le force à sortir en vie" (*84*, 18).[20]

The argument that the expression of one who has suffered as much as he must be valid is the basis for Artaud's account of his fusion of poetry and theater in the "Tête-à-tête" which he presented at the Vieux Colombier Theater in 1947. He is bitterly frustrated that this aspect of his performance was lost in the appreciations of its shock value: "Ce n'est pas le fond qui a frappé le public, la douleur et ses causes, mais la forme, l'atrocité de la voix, le tourment réel de ses attitudes."[21] Despite his disappointment, he expresses satisfaction with the successful "painting" of a pain. He goes on to enumerate the assaults which produced such pain: they include knife wounds, beating with an iron bar, and the torture of shock treatments. But by the mid-1940s, the painful production of poetic meaning has become less important to Artaud than the meaning of pain. The later Artaud is a man with a message which is linked with his suffering both in its source and in the form of retaliation.

A primary characteristic of pain is its demand for an explanation. Having long since exhausted hope for diagnosis by physicians, Artaud turns to metaphysical systems in order to seek the cause of his suffering. Even in the early 1930s, Artaud's writings discuss pain as being inherent in the order of the world, an order which is perpetual conflict. Cruelty and its consequent suffering are corollaries of the intrinsic evil of a world in which "le mal est la loi permanente" (IV, 124).[22] The double sense of *mal*—evil and pain—is another linguistic "cause" which implies a link between the nature of the world and the human condition.

Artaud is always more concerned with his personal suffering than with that of the general population, and his mental process is deductive: "j'ai mal" ("I hurt") implies "on m'a fait mal" ("someone has hurt me"), which inevitably leads Artaud to the conclusion that "on est malfaiteur" ("one is an evildoer/an inflictor of pain"). An example of this reasoning appears in Artaud's account of his back pain, which gives rise to an explanation of vast metaphysical implications. His account, which involves a stabbing motivated by supernatural forces, is validated by the scar which remains on his back. Like the stigmata of a saint, the traces of painful experiences on Artaud's body point to and verify the philosophy which he promulgates.[23]

Throughout the *Lettres de Rodez,* Artaud blames his suffering on the sexual misdeeds of cabalistic cults which are excluded from public awareness by a conspiracy of silence. Evil beings use his body to sustain themselves, sapping his essential health:

> Ces esprits ne veulent pas être chassés parce que mon corps est bon, et que ma douleur est bonne pour eux et c'est en souffrant de poisons, de comas, de mauvaise nourriture et de privation d'opium que les êtres de mauvais esprits prennent dans le cadavre que je suis. (IX, 209–10)[24]

This activity is responsible not only for his pain, but also for all illness: there would be no maladies in the world were it not for these evil men and spirits. In *Pour en finir avec le jugement de dieu* and other texts written after Artaud's liberation, these evil forces are both inte-riorized and magnified. Pain will not be abolished until man is purified of organs, germs, and God (the three are intrinsically related). Only theater is capable of this purgation, which permits health to reign in the absence of God.

Pain operates a split in human perception, a consciousness of part of the body as being alien; the abolition of pain will come only when the body is a homogeneous entity. The process of cure is a transforma-tion which goes beyond the corporeal status quo; it is not a retreat but an aggression. No longer something intrinsic to Artaud's body, pain is in the end a parasitic quality which is imposed on him from without by others as he continues a process of purgation and purification:

> Cette opération consiste à se jeter tout entier dans
>   l'état de la douleur suprême.
> Or voilà longtemps que je l'ai dépassé et que je ne
>   souffre plus que parce que tous les êtres sont sur
>   moi qui me passent leurs charognes à protéger contre
>   la douleur dont ils ne veulent pas et que c'est la
>   leur que je sens sur moi.
> Morale:
> exterminer minutieusement l'humanité,
> je ne souffrirai plus de rien.[25]

Artaud becomes a virtuoso of pain, taking on all the suffering of humanity. As a Christ figure,[26] he undergoes (in writing) the crucifix-ion which has haunted him since his 1936 trip to the land of the Tarahumaras. The analgesic drugs which Artaud took in quantity after his release from Rodez did not annihilate pain, but removed it from his somatic self-perception. Like the refashioned human body, his pain is a distillation of consummate purity: "La douleur, mon élément" ("Pain, my element").[27]

Pain is, then, the supremely meaningful experience for Artaud, the sole generator of significance which he acknowledges both in his own writing and in the work of other artists. The acuteness of his suffering validates the necessity of his discourse; as he insists to Rivière, the right to speak is accompanied by the duty to reveal the knowledge acquired through the experience of pain. Only meaning derived from pain can shed light on its cause: God, the source of all evil.

Notes and References

Chapter One

1. "I wondered why I was there and what it meant to be there. . . . Slaps, cuffings, reprimands, eternal lectures about anything and everything. . . . That is how I was a child in the scandal of my self" ["Je n'ai jamais rien étudié . . .," *84*, 16 (1948)]. All translations are my own and will follow the French as closely as possible.

2. A poem from this period, "Le Navire mystique," was published in *La Criée*, 15 (August 1922). See *Antonin Artaud: Selected Writings*, ed. Susan Sontag (New York, 1976), pp. 3, 596.

3. "An utterly exceptional being, of that race which produces Baudelaires, Nervals or Nietzsches" [Memoir by Mme Toulouse in *La Tour de Feu*, pp. 63–64 (1968)].

4. See Volumes I and II of Artaud's *Oeuvres complètes* (Paris, 1956, 1961).

5. See Artaud's *Lettres à Génica Athanasiou* (Paris, 1969).

6. Artaud also worked in Germany during this period, playing a variety of secondary film roles. In "Artaud Possessed" (*New York Review of Books*, November 11, 1976, p. 19), Roger Shattuck goes so far as to suggest that Artaud's persona was influenced by the character played by Conrad Veidt in the German film *The Cabinet of Dr. Caligari*. This speculation cannot, of course, be verified, but the great activity in German film of the twenties and thirties must have come to Artaud's attention.

7. "1) because there is no longer anything in it with which to face up to current catastrophic necessities; 2) because it is *immoral*, being built exclusively on profit and money." All references to the Gallimard edition of Artaud's *Oeuvres complètes* will be noted in this manner.

8. "I feel that something important, perhaps sensational can come from all of this."

9. See Artaud's letters to André Breton in *L'Ephémère*, 8 (1954).

10. See Paule Thévenin, "Antonin Artaud dans la vie," *Tel Quel*, 20 (Winter 1965), p. 33; for the suicide theory, see Danièle André-Carraz, *L'Expérience intérieure d'Antonin Artaud* (Paris, 1973), p. 107.

11. "Where the *machine* is / it is always abyss and nothingness / there is a technical interposition which deforms and annihilates / what one has done."

Chapter Two

1. "Does not represent me in any way." *Le Tric-trac du ciel* appears at the end of the revised edition of Volume I, pp. 251–61.

2. "I suffer from a terrible illness of the mind. My thought abandons me in every degree. From the simple fact of thought to the exterior fact of its materialization in words. Words, forms of sentences, inner directions of thought, simple reactions of the mind, I am constantly pursuing my intellectual being. So when *I can grasp a form*, however imperfect it may be, I fix it, out of the fear of losing the whole thought. I am beneath myself, I know it, I suffer from it, but do not consent to it in fear of not dying completely."

3. "Their soul is not physiologically affected, not substantially."

4. "I am a man who has suffered greatly in my mind, and in this sense I have the *right* to speak."

5. For more extensive discussions of Artaud's cosmic vision, see Eric Sellin, *The Dramatic Concepts of Antonin Artaud* (Chicago, 1968).

6. "I would like to do a Book that disturbs people, that is like an open door and leads them where they would never have agreed to go, a door simply opening upon reality."

7. "To burn questions."

8. "Now we must speak of the disincorporation of reality, of this sort of rupture, one could say, applied to multiplying itself between things and the feeling they produce on our minds, the place they are to take."

9. "The mind is sure. It really has one foot in this world. The grenade, the belly, the breasts are like proofs attesting to reality."

10. "Uplift my abasement, balance what falls, reunite what is separated, reconstitute what is destroyed."

11. This text is a parody of Armand Salacrou's *Boule de verre (Glass Ball)*.

12. "The virgin! ah, that's what he was looking for!"

13. "For we are *solely* in the Mind."

14. "It participates in the general detachment of Paolo Uccello's mind and perhaps nurtures him a little during his life."

15. "*There is only one thing which creates art: the palpability of man's intentions.* It is consciousness which renders truth."

16. In *L'Art et la mort* (1928).

17. For a cogent analysis of the "myth of hairs," see Mary Ann Caws, "Artaud's Myth of Motion," *The Inner Theater of Recent French Poetry* (Princeton, 1972), pp. 138–40.

18. In *En compagnie d'Antonin Artaud* (Paris, 1974), Jacques Prevel reports a conversation in which Artaud insists that these poems were the last time he used "poetic form" (p. 34).

19. "With me hound-god, and his tongue / which like an arrow pierces the crust / of the double vaulted dome / of the itching earth."

"Eyes rage, tongues turn / the heavens surge into our nostrils."

"On the tables the idolized sky / braces itself, and the delicate sex // dips an icy tongue / into each hole, into each place / that the advancing sky leaves behind."

20. "And I told you: no works, no language, no word, nothing / Nothing, unless it be fine Nerve Scale / A sort of incomprehensible and upright stance in the middle of everything in the mind."

21. "There are a few of us in this epoch who wanted to reach things, to create in ourselves spaces for life, spaces which were not in space."

22. "Like all women you judge with your sex and not with your thought."

23. "All the terms I choose for thinking are for me TERMS in the literal sense of the word, real terminations, ends of my mental   . I am really LOCALIZED by my terms . . . I am really paralyzed by my terms, by a series of terminations."

24. "Nothing touches me, nothing interests me except what addresses itself *directly* to my flesh."

25. Most of these first appeared in Artaud's private publication *Bilboquet*.

26. "All the systems I will be able to erect will never equal my cries, those of a man busy remaking his life."

27. "*Someone* has suicided me, that is. But what would you think of an *anterior suicide?*"

28. "A somber and untranslatable science is piled up, full of subterranean swamps, concave edifices, a frozen agitation."

29. On the title, Artaud remarked nearly twenty years later to Prevel, "C'est l'art qui produit / la mort" ("It is art which produces / death," p. 54).

30. See I, 396.

31. "Death is not beyond the domain of the mind; within certain limits, it is knowable and approachable by a certain sensibility." . . . "You were dead and here you are again finding yourself alive—ONLY THIS TIME YOU ARE ALONE."

32. "I cannot get used to the idea that you are submitted to the conditions of Space, of Time, that corporeal necessities weight on you."

33. "All these ebbings begin with me. . . . The world foams there like the rocky sea, and I with the ebbtide of love. . . . This fire must begin with me."
"The earth is a mother under the ice of fire."
"The fearful point of force which breaks in a totally blue clashing."

34. The other text, "Uccello le Piol," is discussed on pp. 29–30.

35. "But Heloise also has legs. The loveliest thing is that she has legs. She also has this thing like a sailor's sextant, around which all magic turns and grazes, this thing like a recumbent blade."

36. "Pleasure makes a cutting and mystical music on the cutting edge of a sharpened dream."

37. "Poor man! Poor Antonin Artaud! He is indeed this impotent man who scales the stars, who strives to confront his weakness with the cardinal point of the elements. . . . If he could create as many elements, furnish at least a metaphysics of disasters, the beginning would be the collapse!"

38. "I wanted her to be mirrored with flowers, with little volcanoes attached to her armpits, and especially this bitter almond lava which was in the center of her upright body."

39. "The abortions of the human mind at these exhausted thresholds of the soul which man's mind never reaches."

40. "Soon there was only an enormous mountain of ice on which a head of blonde hair hung."

41. "Ah medicine, here is the man who has TOUCHED danger. You have won, psychiatry, you have WON and he goes beyond you." The "Lettre aux médecins-chefs des asiles de fous," which appeared in the same number of *La Révolution Surréaliste*, is no longer attributed to Artaud; it has been deleted from the revised edition of Volume I.

42. "That each man may wish to consider nothing beyond his deep sensitivity, his intimate self, that is for me the point of view of the integral Revolution."

43. See Supplement to Volume I, p. 88.

Chapter Three

1. The most interesting ones are included in Artaud's "Tête-à-tête," a dramatic reading presented on January 13, 1947; other dramatic poems include *Pour en finir avec le jugement de dieu*, a radio performance text of 1947, and "Le Théâtre de la cruauté," a 1948 poem.

2. For discussions of influences, see Henri Gouhier, *Antonin Artaud et l'essence du théâtre* (Paris, 1974), and Alain Virmaux, *Antonin Artaud et le Théâtre* (Paris, 1970).

3. In the revised edition of Artaud's *Oeuvres complètes*, it appears in the second volume.

4. "Transsubstantiation of life."

5. In fact, Aron resigned in 1928 after the *Dream Play* affair.

6. "Must be quite persuaded that we are capable of making him scream."

7. The French verb *répéter* means both "to repeat" and "to rehearse."

8. "Simply with regard to the displacement of air that its enunciation provokes."

9. "It is certain that if I had created a theater, what I would have done would be as little related to what we are accustomed to calling theater as the performance of some obscenity resembles an ancient religious mystery."

10. See Chapter 1 for a more detailed discussion of these controversies; further analysis is found in Naomi Greene, *Antonin Artaud: Poet Without Words* (New York, 1970).

11. "By *specifically theatrical means* to contribute to the ruin of the theater as it presently exits in France."

12. All the cuttings which compose this dialogue are taken from the newspaper *L'Argus* (cf. II, p. 86).

13. "[Vitrac] wanted to wear out this shuddering side which is crumbling

not only from sentiment but also from human thought, to bring to light the deep and eternal antithesis between the servitude of our situation and our material functions and our quality as angels and pure minds."

14. At this time Artaud was a member of Charles Dullin's theatrical company, L'Atelier; Dullin's interest in Japanese theater may well have influenced this text.

15. The theme of incest between siblings or parent and child appears as early as the late 1910s in the poem "Rêve" ("Dream," I, p. 331), and emerges as a major motivation in *Les Cenci*.

16. It was apparently a satire of commercial cinema.

17. The sexual ambiguity of Harlequin recalls Apollinaire's *Les Mamelles de Tirésias*.

18. "The paroxysms of a violent material action;" "No free will. Classify Evil. Understand its destiny. Man, a plaything of God, Plaything of himself."

19. "To shatter language in order to touch life is to create or remake theater; and the important thing is not to believe that this act must remain sacred, that is, reserved. Rather, the important thing is to believe that not just anyone can do it, and that a preparation is necessary."

20. "And by this double I mean the great magical agent of which the theater, through its forms, is only the figuration waiting to become the transfiguration."

21. "Now it is a matter of knowing whether, in Paris, before the heralded cataclysms occur, sufficient means of realization—financial or other—can be found in order to allow such a theater to live; and it will hold on in every way because it is the future. Or whether a little real blood will be necessary right away in order to make this cruelty known."

22. Alternative names proposed include "Le Théâtre alchimique" ("Alchemical Theater"), "Métaphysique" ("Metaphysical"), and "de la NRF" ("of the NRF"); see Volume V, *passim*.

23. "A sort of arid moral purity which does not fear to pay for life the price which must be paid."

24. "And so it is that all great Myths are black and every magnificent Fable which tells the masses about the first sexual parturition and the first carnage of essences which appear in creation cannot be imagined outside an atmosphere of carnage, torture and spilt blood."

25. "We are not free. And the sky can still fall on our heads. And theater is made to teach us that first."

26. "And if there is still something infernal and truly accursed in this time, it is to linger artistically over forms, instead of being like martyrs who are burned and who make signs on their stakes."

27. "I propose rigorous, unexpected principles of forbidding and terrible appearance, and at the very moment when you expect to see me justify them I pass on to the next principle."

28. "Metaphysics will be made to reenter the mind through the skin"; "what theater can still take from speech is its capacity to expand beyond

words, to develop in space a dissociating, vibratory action on the sensibilities."

29. "The spectacle will be coded from one end to the other, like a language."

30. Perhaps the title of this play appealed to Artaud because of the suggestion of *ardent* in "Arden" and of *fever* in "Feversham."

31. "A passionate and convulsive life"; "violent rigor [and] extreme condensation of the scenic elements."

32. "If, in today's digestive theater, the nerves, that is, a certain physiological sensitivity, are deliberately set aside, given over to the spectator's individual anarchy, the Theater of Cruelty intends to return to all the old tried and magical means of reaching the sensibility."

33. "There is a movement today to separate theater from all that which is not space, and to return the language of the text to the books which it should never have left. And this language of space acts in turn on the nervous sensitivity, it makes the landscape which spreads around it ripen."

34. In order to demonstrate his acting ability, he included Shakespeare's *Richard II* along with *La Conquête du Mexique* as an example of directorial potential, and several theoretical essays.

35. "A success in the Absolute."

36. "I fear that death will teach me / that in the end I resembled him."

37. "Let us recognize that what has been said need not be said any more; that an expression is not good twice; does not live twice; that every spoken word is dead and acts only at the moment when it is pronounced, that a used form no longer works, and only invites us to search for another, and that the theater is the only place in the world where a gesture made is not started twice.

38. "Le Théâtre de la cruauté et la clôture de la représentation," *L'Ecriture et la différence* (Paris, 1967), pp. 341–68.

Chapter Four

1. "A culture based on the mind in relation to the organs."

2. "From emptiness toward forms, and from forms [it] reenters the void, in emptiness as in death. Being cultivated is setting forms on fire, burning forms for a living. It is learning to hold oneself erect in the incessant movement of forms which are destroyed one after the other."

3. "Not possible not to find something to answer me."

4. See André Frank, Introduction to *Lettres d'Antonin Artaud à Jean-Louis Barrault* (Paris, 1952), pp. 51–85; Jean-Louis Barrault, "Conviction et malaise du théâtre contemporain," *Cahiers Renaud-Barrault*, 71 (1970).

5. "Where the life of the world is based on the search for the Unity of things, / the history of peoples is the story of the betrayal of this unity."

6. "A sort of conciliation will be made beyond the stupidity of people, / everyone will suddenly discover himself to be great and prophetic, / people will look at *themselves* and will no longer recognize themselves."

7. "Came to Mexico to flee European civilization and culture which are leading us all to Barbary."

8. "Freedom of the Spirit in the Spirit"; "suspended among all forms and hoping only for the wind."

9. This preoccupation with the origin of evil is one link between Artaud and gnosticism; see Susan Sontag, "Reflections: Approaching Artaud," *New Yorker*, May 19, 1973, pp. 39–79.

10. See "La Médecine qui guérit," VIII, pp. 20–21.

11. "Opium, which intervenes between musical form and the memory of the unconscious, allow us . . . to describe the uncertainty of the mind with regard to all that the intelligence names."

12. Jean-Claude Montel, "Pouvoir imposteur," *Change*, 7 (1970), pp. 179–84.

13. Georges Charbonnier, *Antonin Artaud* (Paris, 1959), p. 209.

14. "True or not, the character of Heliogabalus lives, I think, even in his depths, whether they be those of the historical personage Heliogabalus or of a personage who is myself", "just the same, I wind up rejoining myself in the details of many, many passages, and in the conception of the central figure in which I have described myself."

15. The derivations of the name appear on VII, pp. 22, 96–101.

16. "Principles only have value for the thinking mind, and when it thinks, but outside the thinking mind, a principle is reduced to nothing."

17. "At the origin of their beliefs, there is a terrible effort not to think as men, in order to maintain contact with all of creation, that is, with divinity."

18. "Everywhere fullness, excess, abundance, immoderation. Generosity and the purest pity which come to counterbalance a spasmodic cruelty."

19. "Order, Disorder / Unity, Anarchy / Poetry, Dissonance / Rhythm, Discordance / Grandeur, Puerility / Generosity, Cruelty."

20. "An idea of the alchemical transformation of feelings into forms and forms into feelings . . . an idea of purification."

21. "Filter for human blood"; "spasmodic O of heaven."

22. "The blood of the sun rises as dew in his head, and each solar dewdrop becomes an energy and an idea."

23. "Magic monotheism which is not just of the word, but of action."

24. "The necessity of madness throughout Western history is linked to this gesture of decision which detaches from the background noise and from its continuous monotony a significant language which is transmitted and comes to fruition in time; in short, it is linked to the possibility of history." Michel Foucault, *Folie et déraison: Histoire de la folie à l'âge classique* (Paris, 1961), p. vi.

25. This fragmentary text, which appeared after an eighteen-year delay, continues to be a subject of some controversy. See the notes to *Satan*, VIII, pp. 398–400.

26. "Refraction of Satanic thought."

27. "For I pull something out of nothing and not *Nothing* from something."

28. "And with a single movement here is the system, frozen, showing its arcanas which are similar to the arcades of a bridge that would connect two immensities."

Chapter Five

1. Artaud was neither the first nor the last European to seek cultural renewal in Mexico. Perhaps his best-known predecessor was D. H. Lawrence, whose novel *The Plumed Serpent* (1926) is the product of his Mexican experience. After Artaud, a number of his Surrealist associates lived in Mexico during World War II. Benjamin Péret, who was fascinated by the indigenous culture, wrote the beautiful "Air mexicain" (1944) in celebration of its past and potential future: yet Péret's approach to Mexican civilization was in its own terms rather than in those of the universal culture sought by Artaud.

2. "Every true civilization has its base in astrology and knows how to restrict to the minimum its catastrophes and its crimes."

3. "Perhaps it is a baroque idea for a European to go to Mexico to seek out the living bases of a culture the notion of which seems to be crumbling here; but I confess that this idea obsesses me; there is in Mexico, tied to the soil, lost in the flows of volcanic lava, vibrating in Indian blood, the magic reality of a culture which would doubtless take very little to relight its fires materially."

4. "Any civilization for which the body is on one side and the mind on the other soon risks seeing come apart the bonds which unite these two dissimilar realities."

5. "I came to Mexico to seek a new idea of man."

6. For details, see IX, pp. 241–58.

7. "Led by the *Invisible* just as I feel that all my life is *actually* conducted."

8. "This archeology is also a teleology and an eschatology; dream of a full and immediate presence closing history; transparence and nondivision of a parousia, suppression of contradiction and of difference." Jacques Derrida, *De la grammatologie* (Paris, 1968), p. 168.

9. "Christ is what I have always abominated the most."

10. "That is to tell you that it is not Jesus Christ whom I went to look for among the Tarahumaras but myself, I, Mr. Antonin Artaud, born September 4, 1896, in Marseilles at 4, rue du Jardin des Plantes, from a uterus where I had no business being and with which I had had nothing to do even before, because that is no way to be born, to be copulated and masturbated for nine months by the membrane, the shining membrane which devours without teeth as the UPANISHADS say, and I know that I was born otherwise."

11. "The figure of extreme operations by which MAN THE FATHER, NEITHER MAN NOR WOMAN created everything."

12. "A Ritual of creation and [one] which explains how things *are* in the Void and it in the Infinite and how they emerged from it into Reality and were made."

13. "For I thought I saw in this Dance the point in which the universal unconscious is ill."

14. J. E. Cirlot, *A Dictionary of Symbols* (New York, 1962), p. 233.

15. "On the side where my spleen was, there was hollowed out an immense void which was painted gray and pink like the seashore. And at the bottom of this void appeared the form of a washed-up root, a sort of J which would have had superimposed at its top three branches of an E, as sad and shining as an eye. Some flames came out of the left eye of the J and, passing behind it, seemed to push everything to the right, on the side where my liver was, but far beyond it. I saw no more of it and everything vanished, or it was I who vanished upon returning to everyday reality. In any case I had seen, it seems, the very Spirit of Ciguri."

16. This passage recalls the confusing metaphysical speculation of the chapter entitled "La Guerre des principes" in *Héliogabale*.

17. "I was ready for all the burns, and I awaited the first fruits of the burn, in view of a combustion which would soon be generalized."

18. "The land of the Tarahumaras is full of signs, forms, natural effigies which do not seem to have been born by chance, as if the gods whose presence is felt everywhere here had wished to displays their powers in these strange signatures in which the figure of man is hunted on every hand."

19. "A history of childbirth in war, a history of genesis and chaos."

20. "The Tarahumaras have sown this inhabited Sierra which blows a metaphysical wind with signs, perfectly conscious, intelligent and concerted signs."

21. See also his letter to Paulhan of February 4, 1937 (IX, pp. 121–28).

22. "The Signs of a language based on the very form of breath when it frees itself in sonorities."

23. "And it seems strange to me that the primitive Tarahumaran people, whose rites and thought are older than the Flood, could have already possessed this science well before the Grail Legend appeared, well before the Rosicrucian sect was formed."

24. "On the Tarahumara mountain, everything speaks only of the Essential, that is, of the principles according to which nature was formed; and everything lives only for these principles: men, storms, wind, silence, sun."

25. "Nature produced dancers in their circle just as she produces corn in its circle and signs in the forests."

26. "Here geometric space is alive; it has produced what is best, that is, Man."

27. "The idea of this ritual came to them from the same fabulous and prehistoric source."

28. A more graphic description of their squalor appears in the letter to Paulhan of February 4, 1937.

29. There are two texts entitled "Tutuguri"; the second is part of the sequence prepared for the radio broadcast *Pour en finir avec le jugement de dieu (To End God's Judgment)*; see IX, pp. 251–52.

30. "The ritual of the black night and of the *eternal* death of the sun."

31. " . . . the approaching horse carries on it the trunk of a man/a naked man who is brandishing/not a cross/but a staff of wood of iron/attached to a giant horseshoe/through which his whole body passes,/his body cut with a gash of blood,/and the horseshoe is there,/like the jaws of an iron collar/which the man had taken from the gash of blood."

32. See Manuel Cano de Castro, "Rencontre d'Antonin Artaud avec les tarots," *K*, 102 (1948), pp. 119–23.

33. "My name must disappear"; "in a little while I will be dead or else in such a situation that at any rate I will not need a name."

34. "The Tortured One has become for everyone the Recognized One, THE REVEALED ONE."

35. "I say what I have seen and what I believe; and anyone who says I did not see what I have seen, I tear his head off right now."

36. "The Right of which I am thinking is Man's Right and not stupid Reaction."

37. "We are threatened with slavery because Nature is going to fall back down on us."

38. The cane and sword are, respectively, the "cane of Saint Patrick" which was given to Artaud by the wife of the painter Kristian Tony and a dagger which was given to him in Havana.

39. "A cycle of the world is finished."

40. "On July 25, 1937, the Macrocosm met the Earth."

41. Artaud dedicated a copy of *Les Nouvelles Révélations* to Adolf Hitler, whom he believed he had met. For details, see VII, pp. 429–30.

Chapter Six

1. See Gaston Ferdière, "J'ai soigné Antonin Artaud," reprinted in *La Tour de feu*, 112 (1971), pp. 24–33, and the irate rebuttal by Paule Thévenin, "Antonin Artaud dans la vie," *Tel Quel*, 20 (1965), pp. 25–40.

2. "Sur *Les Chimères*" was first published in *Tel Quel*, 22 (1965), pp. 3–13; it is included in *Oeuvres complètes*, XI, pp. 184–201.

3. Georges Le Breton, "La Clé des *Chimères*: L'Alchimie," *Fontaine*, 44 (1945). Le Breton wrote a second article on Nerval for *Fontaine*, "L'Alchimie dans *Aurélia*; 'Les Mémorables,'" (1945), but Artaud only refers to the first one. Artaud's editor states that "Sur *les Chimères*" was to have been published as an article, but that this project was abandoned (XI, p. 331).

4. More recently, Henri Meschonnic has denounced occultist criticism of Nerval in his "Essai sur la poétique de Nerval," *Europe*, 516 (1972), p.7.

5. "In the tumefying scab of his heart of an immortal suicide, there are born beings who come bellowing into the foreground their drama of the tragedy of their will for clarity."

6. "This spirit of eternal laziness which, always, before pain, and in fear of getting too close to it, I mean of *knowing* Gérard de Nerval's soul, as one knows the buboes of a plague . . . has taken refuge in source criticism."

7. "Gérard de Nerval, from the heart of his spiritual tumors, managed to make beings live, beings taken by him from alchemy, which he reclaimed from Myths, and saved from burial in the Tarot."

8. "Strange and marvelous machines of the consciousness."

9. "Gérard de Nerval, hanged one morning and nothing more."

10. "Proof of the meaning of the verses of *Les Chimères* cannot be made by Mythology . . . but solely by diction . . . on the condition that they are *spat out* freshly and at every reading.—For it is then that their hieroglyphs become clear."

11. "Scarcely had she opened her mouth than he stopped her: 'Shut up! if you persist in forbidding me to recite Gérard de Nerval's verses, I will immediately change you into a flat-headed [i.e., poisonous] snake,'" Paule Thévenin, "Antonin Artaud dans la vie," *Tel Quel*, 20 (1965), p.29.

12. "All that which is not a tetanus of the soul or does not come from a tetanus of the soul like the poems of Baudelaire or Edgar Poe is not true and cannot be received into poetry"; "I love poems . . . of those tortured by language who are at a loss in their writings"; "A poem which does not come from pain bores me, a poem created with all the superfluities of being . . . exasperates me."

13. "There is not one of our words which does not live in our mouth *unglued from heaven*," "Lettre à Adrienne Monnier," *K, Revue de Poésie*, 1–2 (1948), p.114.

14. "A poem which is outside of the heart, outside of the anguish and the sobbing heart, a poem which has not been *suffered*."

15. "Pure language with meaning beyond the grammatical."

16. "Anguish this old servant of pain, this buried shrew's sex which takes her worms out of her illness."

17. "I know not which priest . . . diverted him toward the frightful pain that his secular and premeditated magic made up, but which, in fact, had never existed," in "Coleridge le traître," *K, Revue de Poésie*, 1–2 (1948), p.96. This essay will be referred to in the text as *K*.

18. "For *after*, says 'poematic,' after will come the time of blood. / Since *ema*, in Greek, means blood, and po-ema must mean: / after / the blood / the blood after. / First let us make *poem*, with blood."

19. "Yes, beneath the tourniquet of pain, there is a blood which comes out, one hour for the clot thawed of the shadows, and which is itself this true child without sex, born outside the slimy parturitions of sex which were only the throat and the nail of a primitive strangling."

20. The story appears in *Cahiers de la compagnie théâtrale Madeleine Renaud-Jean-Louis Barrault*, 22–23 (1958); the (apparently) accurate account of the writing of this text is given in the notes to the Gallimard edition, XIII, pp.300–302.

21. "A man who preferred to go crazy, in the sense in which it is socially understood, rather than forfeit a certain superior idea of human honor . . . a man whom society did not wish to hear and wanted to keep from emitting unbearable truths."

22. "We can speak of the good mental health of Van Gogh who, in his whole life, cooked only one of his hands and did no more, for the rest, than cut off his left ear one time / in a world where some vagina cooked in green sauce or the sex of a flagellated, rabid newborn is eaten every day."

23. "Van Gogh did not die from a state of actual delirium but from having been physically the arena of a problem about which, since its origins, the iniquitous spirit of this humanity has *fought*, / That of the predominance of flesh over spirit, or of the body over flesh or of the spirit over both." It is interesting to note that Artaud distinguishes between "flesh" and "the body"; the latter includes the organs, which he will reject as valid components of human anatomy.

24. "Combed by Van Gogh's nail, /landscapes show their hostile flesh, / the forge of their disemboweled folds, /which some alien force is, on the other hand, in the midst of metamorphosing."

25. "For it is, however, certainly after a conversation with Dr. Gachet that Van Gogh, as if it were nothing, went back to his room and committed suicide."

26. "For the separating nail criterion is not a question of breadth or cramp, but of the simple force of the first."

27. "The most authentic painter of all painters, the only one who did not want to go beyond painting . . . the only one who, on the other hand, absolutely the only one, absolutely went beyond painting, the inert act of representing nature, in order to make a turning force well up over it in this exclusive representation of nature and element torn from the very heart."

28. "Van Gogh thought that one must know how to deduce myth from the most down-to-earth things in life."

29. "For aren't we all, like poor Van Gogh himself, society's suicides."

30. Artaud defines "La culture turque" in the text and more extensively in an earlier draft (pp. 193–95) as it relates to Turkey; since his mother's (and less immediately, his father's) background was Greek, this pejorative phrase may derive from political animosities.

31. "He who does not smell of cooked bomb and compressed vertigo is not worthy of being alive."

32. "One day Van Gogh's painting, armed with both fever and good health /will return to throw into the air the dust of a caged world which his heart could no longer bear."

Chapter Seven

1. They are widely dispersed in published and unpublished sources; Volume XIV, which should contain a number of these shorter texts, is not published at the time of this writing.

2. Such writing may be found in Phillipe Sollers, "L'Etat Artaud," *Artaud*, ed. Phillipe Sollers (Paris, 1973) and Georges Charbonnier, *Essai sur Antonin Artaud* (Paris, 1959).

3. For an exhaustive explication of the title *Artaud le Mômo*, see Paule Thévenin, "Entendre/Voir /Lire," *Tel Quel*, 40 (1970), pp. 67–99.

4. "The spirit anchored / screwed in me / by the psycholibidinous thrust / of heaven / is the one who thinks / all temptation / all desire / all inhibition." The last four lines are invented language and therefore are not translated.

5. "I will be fifty years old next September 4, which does not mean that I was born in Marseilles on September 4, 1896, as my civil status holds, / but I remember having passed through there one night at the pussy-owner hour / I remember having created, myself, my own *incarnation* there that night, instead of having received it from a father and a mother."

6. "Interference of action / transfer by deportation / reestablishment outside excision / cutting off of clogging / foundation finally / in the non-outside."

7. "It is not just that doctors favor magic by their inopportune and hybrid therapies / they actually do it. / If there had been no doctors / there would never have been sick people."

8. *"You are no longer there / but nothing leaves you / you have conserved everything / except yourself // and what does it matter since / the world / is there. // The / world / but that is no longer I / And what does it matter / says the Bardo / it is I."*

9. See XII, pp. 292–93. The Gallimard edition has been corrected and is augmented with the usual group of earlier states of the text.

10. "The hole of emptiness, the acrid empty hole, where boils the cycle of the red lice / cycle of the solar red lice / completely white in the network of veins of the one two."

11. "Why two of them / and why from TWO?"; "and that means that war / will replace the father-mother."

12. "Interloper between ji and cri / contracted into / jiji-cricri."

13. "That is how they / drew out of me / papa and mama / and the frying of ji into / Cri / . . . which gave life / to Jizo-cri."

14. "Don't you see that the false son-in-law / is jizi-cri / already known in Mexico / well before his flight to Jerusalem on an ass, / and the crucifixion of Artaud at Golgotha. / Artaud / who knew that there is no spirit / just a body."

15. "For I was an Inca but not a king . . . TILI / pinches you / in the *falzourchte* / of all gold, / in the rout / of your body."

16. "I, Antonin Artaud, I am my son, my father, my mother, and I; / leveler of the imbecile periplus where begetting runs itself through / the periplus of papa-mama / and the child."

17. "Do not tire yourself more than necessary, it it enough to found a culture on the fatigue of your bones"; "bone by bone / the sempiternal equalization returned."

18. "As if time / were not fried / were not this fried cooking / of all the crumbled ones / of the threshold, / reembarked in their coffins."

19. Henceforth referred to as *Judgment.*

20. "Bursts the cross so that the spaces of space can never meet nor cross."

21. "Because they squeezed me / up to my body / and up to the body // and that is when / I made everything explode / because my body / is never touched."

22. See notes, XIII, p. 349.

23. "There is nothing existent and real / but exterior physical life / and everything that flees it and turns from it / is but the limbo world of the demons."

24. "Who am I? / Where do I come from? / I am Antonin Artaud / and let me say it / as I know how to say it / immediately / you will see my current body / fly into pieces / and gather itself back up / in ten thousand ways / notorious / a new body / in which you will never / be able to / forget me."

Chapter Eight

1. "I suffer from a frightful illness of the spirit."

2. "I am a man who has suffered greatly, and on this count I have the *right* to speak."

3. Maurice Blanchot, "Artaud," *Le Livre à venir* (Paris, 1959), p. 62; "Might extreme thought and extreme suffering open the same horizon? Might suffering, finally, be thinking?"

4. Tristan Tzara affirms that the continuity in Artaud's work is provided by "la douleur projetée sur la vie mentale" ("suffering projected onto mental life"); "Antonin Artaud, le désespoir de la connaissance," *Les Lettres françaises*, 201 (1948), p. 1. Marthe Robert sees Artaud's life as a continual rebellion against "l'intolérable scandale de la souffrance" ("the intolerable scandal of suffering"); "Je suis cet insurgé du corps . . ." ("I am this insurgent of the body"), *Cahiers de la compagnie théâtrale Madeleine Renaud-Jean-Louis Barrault*, 69 (1969), p. 37. For other discussions of pain in Artaud's life, see Danièle André-Carraz, *Antonin Artaud: L'Expérience intérieure* (Paris, 1973) and Alain Virmaux, *Antonin Artaud et le théâtre* (Paris, 1970), pp. 19–21.

5. See Thomas Szasz, *Pain and Pleasure* (New York, 1957).

6. "An unforeseen and sudden electricity"; "these profound tornadoes."

7. "It remains nonetheless that they do not suffer and that I suffer, not only in the spirit, but in the flesh and in my soul every day."

8. "Words are a silt which is illuminated not from the angle of being, but from the angle of its anguish."

9. "I am the master of my pain. Any man is the judge, and the exclusive judge, of the quantity of physical pain, or even of mental vacuity, which he can honestly tolerate."

10. "That my illness has retreated or advanced, the question for me is not there, it is in my pain."

11. Antonin Artaud, *Lettres à Génica Athanasiou* (Paris, 1968), p. 20. Henceforth referred to in the text as *LG*.

12. "But there is one thing / which is some thing / a single thing / which is some thing / and which I feel / in that it wants to GET OUT: / the presence / of my bodily pain."

13. "I have chosen the domain of pain and of shadow, as others have chosen that of radiance and of the piling up of matter."

14. "The idea of suffering is greater than the idea of cure, the idea of life."

15. See Artaud's letter to Soulié de Morant, I, p. 319.

16. "In the state of degeneration where we are, metaphysics will be made to reenter the mind by the skin."

17. "Like a pain which, as it grows in intensity and deepens, multiplies its avenues and its wealth in every circle of sensitivity."

18. In *84*, 16 (1950), pp. 12–18.

19. "Mr. colic, Mr. cramp, Mr. nausea, Mr. vertigo, Mr. spanking, Mr. ear-boxing"; "where being is only healthy in the illness of being," *ibid.*, pp. 12, 18.

20. "Blessed be all illness, for illness sounds being and forces it to come out into life."

21. "It is not the content which struck the public, pain and its causes, but the form, the atrocity of the voice, the real torment of its attitudes," *K, Revue de la Poésie*, 1–2 (1948), p. 110.

22. "Evil is the permanent law."

23. See IX, p. 199 for this detailed account.

24. "These spirits do not want to be chased off because my body is good, and my pain is good for them and it is by suffering from poisons, comas, bad food and deprivation of opium that the beings of the evil spirits take hold of the cadaver that I am."

25. "This operation consists of throwing oneself completely into the state of supreme pain. / It has now been a long time since I went beyond it completely and I only continue to suffer because all the beings are upon me handing over their carcasses to me to protect against the pain which they do not want and which is theirs, pain that I feel upon myself. / Moral: / minutely exterminate humanity, / I will no longer suffer from anything," "Lettre aux balinais," *Tel Quel*, 46 (1971), p. 14.

26. It should be noted that Artaud considers his status to be superior to that of Jesus, whom he brands repeatedly as a fraud.

27. "Lettre aux balinais," p. 14.

Selected Bibliography

PRIMARY SOURCES

1. Editions

Oeuvres complètes. 14 Volumes (I–XIII and Supplement to Volume I). The definitive text with notes and variants; many short, later texts should appear in Volume XIV. Paris: Gallimard, 1956–71.

Lettres à Génica Atanasiou. Paris: Gallimard, 1969.

Lettres d'Antonin Artaud à Jean-Louis Barrault. Paris: Bordas, 1952.

"Lettres à André Breton." *L'Emphémère*, 8 (1954). These three collections of important correspondence do not appear in the *Oeuvres complètes*.

2. Translations

Antonin Artaud: Selected Writings. Edited, with an introduction by Susan Sontag. Translations by Helen Weaver. New York: Farrar, Straus and Giroux, 1976. The best anthology for American readers; outstanding introductory essay.

SECONDARY SOURCES

1. Books

BRAU, JEAN-LOUIS. *Antonin Artaud.* Paris: La Table Ronde, 1971. Good biographical data.

CHARBONNIER, GEORGES. *Essai sur Antonin Artaud.* Paris: Seghers, 1959. Difficult, personal appreciation of Artaud in the *Poètes d'aujourd'hui* series.

GOUHIER, HENRI. *Antonin Artaud et l'essence du théâtre.* Paris: Vrin, 1974. Interesting speculation on sources.

GREENE, NAOMI. *Antonin Artaud: Poet Without Words.* New York: Simon and Schuster, 1970. Best study of Artaud in English.

JOSKI, DANIEL. *Artaud.* Paris: Editions Universitaires, 1970. General survey, more objective than most.

SELLIN, ERIC. *The Dramatic Concepts of Antonin Artaud.* Chicago: University of Chicago Press, 1968. Theater in religious and ritual context.

SOLLERS, PHILIPPE, ed. *Artaud.* Colloque de Cérisy. Paris: Union Générale d'Editions, 1973. Articles by Sollers, Kristeva, *et al.*

VIRMAUX, ALAIN. *Antonin Artaud et le théâtre.* Paris: Seghers, 1970. Strong factual study.

2. Special Issues of Journals

Cahiers de la compagnie théâtrale Madeleine Renaud–Jean-Louis Barrault,
  22–30 (May 1958), reprinted 69 (1969).
K, 1–2 (1948).
Magazine littéraire, 61 (February 1972).
84, 1–2 (1948).

3. Articles and Chapters

BLANCHOT, MAURICE. "La Cruelle raison poétique (rapace besoin d'envol)"
  in *L'Entretien infini*. Paris: Gallimard, 1969, 432–38.
CAWS, MARY ANN. "Artaud's Myth of Motion" in *The Inner Theater of
  Recent French Poetry*. Princeton: Princeton University Press, 1972,
  125–40.
CHIAROMONTE, NICOLA. "Antonin Artaud et sa double idée du théâtre."
  Preuves, 205 (1968), 8–17.
DERRIDA, JACQUES. "La Parole soufflée" in *L'Ecriture el la différence*. Paris:
  Editions du Seuil, 1967, 253–92.
————. "Le Théâtre de la cruauté et la clôture de la représentation" in
  L'Ecriture et la différence, 341–68.
KOCH, STEPHEN. "On Artaud." *Tri-Quarterly*, 6 (1966), 29–37.
LAPORTE, ROGER. "Antonin Artaud ou la pensée au supplice." *Le Nouveau
  Commerce*, 12 (1968), 20–36.
LYONS, JOHN D. "Artaud: Intoxication and Its Double." *Yale French Studies*,
  50 (1974), 120–29.
THÉVENIN, PAULE. "Antonin Artaud dans la vie." *Tel Quel*, 20 (1965), 25–40.
————. "Entendre/Voir/Lire." *Tel Quel*, 39 (1969), 3–29, and 40 (1970),
  67–99.

Index